The Food Processor Cookb

Carol Bowen is a freelance home ecc
contributed to the national press and
acted as consultant to manufacturers of food and kitchenware, done
photographic styling for advertising and books and worked as cookery
consultant for TV-AM's *X-Cel Diet* with Diana Dors. Her other cookery
books include *The Microwave Cookbook*, also published by Pan, and
Versatile Vegetables (Octopus) which won the 1984 Bejam Cookery Book
of the Year Award. Carol Bowen is married and lives with her husband
and young daughter in Surrey.

Other cookery books available in Pan

Kathy Barnes **The Infra-red Cookbook**
Mrs Beeton's Cookery for All
Carol Bowen **The Microwave Cookbook**
Arto Der Haroutounian **Middle Eastern Cookery**
Gail Duff's Vegetarian Cookbook
Theodora FitzGibbon **Crockery Pot Cooking   Irish Traditional Food**
A Taste of . . . series
Michel Guérard's Cuisine Minceur
Rosemary Hume and Muriel Downes **The Best of Cordon Bleu**
Cordon Bleu Book of Jams, Preserves and Pickles
Claire Loewenfeld and Philippa Back **Herbs for Health and Cookery**
Caroline Mackinlay **The Preserving Book**
Maurice Messegué and Madeleine Peter **A Kitchen Herbal**
Elisabeth Orsini **The Book of Pies**
Marguerite Patten **Learning to Cook**
Roger Phillips **Wild Food**
V. V. Pokhlebkin **Russian Delight**
Evelyn Rose **The Complete International Jewish Cookbook**
Katie Stewart **Shortcut Cookbook   The Times Calendar Cookbook**
The Times Cookery Book
Rita Springer **Caribbean Cookbook**
Marika Hanbury Tenison's Freezer Cookbook
Karen Wallace **The Pan Picnic Guide**

Carol Bowen

The Food Processor Cookbook

Pan Original
Pan Books London and Sydney

First published 1985 by Pan Books Ltd,
Cavaye Place, London SW10 9PG
9 8 7 6 5 4 3 2 1
© Carol Bowen 1985
Illustrations © Kim Palmer
ISBN 0 330 28777 X
Photoset by Parker Typesetting Service, Leicester
Printed by Cox & Wyman Ltd, Reading

Contents

Introduction

I call them kitchen wizards, for they seem quite magical in their ability to chop, slice, grate or blend foods in seconds before my very eyes. Sturdy and practical, my processor has now become indispensable – leaving me to wonder how I coped for years without its help. A true friend, it has enabled me to revive and restore those old time-consuming favourites to the menu – silky-smooth vegetable soups, crusty-brown home-baked bread, 'real' meatloaves and hamburgers made with ingredients that I have inspected first hand, and delicious ice creams, sorbets and fools.

Don't be fooled into thinking that a processor is just another blender – it is much more than that. What blender can slice vegetables for salads, prepare pastry in seconds, whizz up a cocktail in the time it takes to say cheers, grate cheese without fear of shaved knuckles and knead bread dough faster than a master baker?

Food processors do, however, vary in their appearance, power, capacity, attachments, capabilities and price. It is with these thoughts in mind that *The Food Processor Cookbook* has been written. I hope it will guide you through the maze of models on the market and enable you to make a wise choice to suit your needs and lifestyle. That achieved, I hope you will try out a few of the tried and tested recipes on your own model and enjoy with me the splendours of tasty, quickly-prepared and tempting food.

During the preparation of this book many friends, colleagues and manufacturers, too many to mention by name, gave their valued opinions and help. Thanks must go to them and to Philips Electrical, Kenwood and Magimix for information and machines supplied for testing. For typing and assistance I would like to thank Claire James and Gail Ashton, for recipe testing Lyn Rutherford and for invaluable help and constructive advice I am grateful to Annie Jackson, my editor at Pan.

Unquestionably, the most useful help came from my husband Peter and very young daughter Lucy who tried many whizzed and whirred foods in a short time and whose grins and grimaces held the key to recipe inclusion. I hope you will enjoy our choice.

Carol Bowen

All about food processors

Food processors are, without doubt, the new wizards of the kitchen, making light work of slicing, chopping, grating, grinding, squeezing, creaming and puréeing almost every conceivable food involved in food preparation and garnishing.

Coupled with speed, and the processor is a great time saver, you have a machine that is hard to beat. The price you pay can, however, be costly, so it pays to look closely at the models available, the attachments and features they provide and any optional extras that can be introduced when budget, enthusiasm and your own family or culinary requirements necessitate.

The type of motor your processor uses will often determine its cost, performance and life span. The Rolls Royce is the direct drive commercial grade induction motor which usually comes with up to a three-year guarantee. Its less expensive but just as powerful counterpart is the series motor, with a guarantee of up to twelve months.

Food processor models

Food processors vary enormously – and so do their features – but it is possible to identify six typical models.

Model A

Perhaps the most popular model available that operates on one speed and does not have an off/on pulse. It comes with four standard attachments: a metal blade, plastic blade, grating disc, and a slicing disc. Some 'A' models also have a whipping blade or 'paddle'. Up to eight optional extras are available.

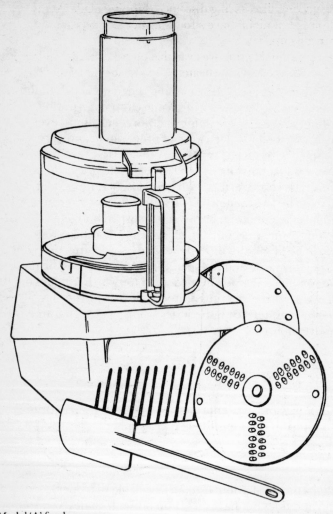

Model 'A' food processor

Model B

A three-speed processor – fast for grating and slicing, medium
for mincing and cake-making, and slow for whisking and
blending. Four attachments are usually supplied – the metal

blade, grating disc, slicing disc and whipping blade. Many examples of model B have a food pusher that acts as a measuring cup.

Many optional extras are available on these models including chipper, whisked sponge beater, and kneader, and one has a soft ice-cream maker.

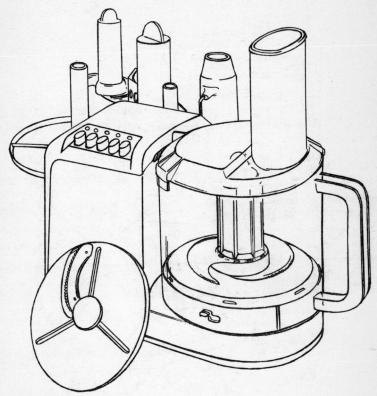

Model 'B' food processor

Model C

A real space-age model with up to six speeds includir g features like touch control, automatic timing and digital display. At least five attachments are supplied as basics – slicing disc, grating disc, metal blade, plastic blade and whipping blade. Also has many optional extras like chipper, juice extractor and citrus press.

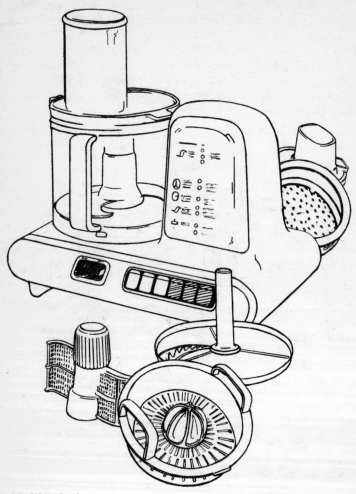

Model 'C' food processor

Model D

Very similar to model A but with refinements, more attachments or extra large capacity. Most processors in the model D range have pulse and continual operation controls – one with an automatic speed selector taking the guesswork out of processing. Has up to six attachments as basic – metal blade, grating disc, slicing disc, chipper, plastic blade, and whipping blade.

Many processors in this category have a larger capacity bowl and more powerful motor, they are available in a selection of colours – and one can be built in to your work-surface.

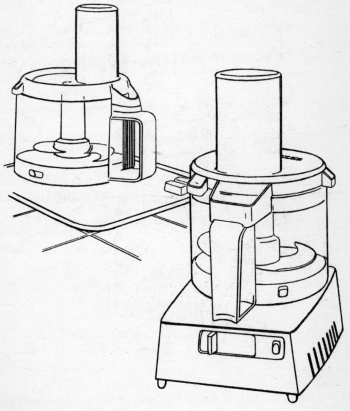

Model 'D' food processors

A food processor and blender combined, both generally with three speed settings and a pulse button. One brand has a special continuous flow facility – so that you can process large quantities

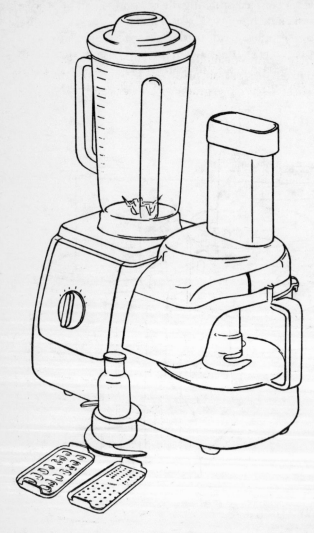

Model 'E' food processor

without having to stop to empty the bowl. This also means that you can direct the food via the spout into the cooking or serving dish. Supplied with up to five basic attachments – including a metal blade and four slicing or grating discs, one of which is a chipper.

Model F

To date there is only one model in this category. It features a one-speed processor with six blades – a metal blade, thick slicer disc, thin slicer disc, coarse grater disc, fine grater disc and chipper.

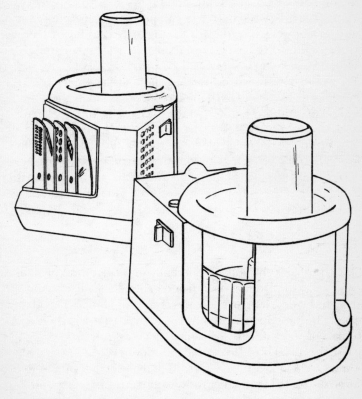

Model 'F' food processor

What makes it unique is its ribbed bowl which reduces scraping down. It is also the only type of processor that has a compartment in the main body of the machine to store blades, discs, and the cord, when not in use.

Attachments

Almost without reservation, every food processor available has three attachments for general use – a metal blade, a grating disc, and a slicing disc. Many standard models also have a plastic blade and a whipping or whisking blade.

Beyond those basic attachments the choices are anything but easy – one manufacturer offers up to eight additional attachments. These additional and luxury attachments take care of specialist food preparation techniques from very fine slicing or grating, chipping, kneading or juicing to ice crushing, Parmesan cheese grating, French fry or julienne slicing, ripple-cutting, and even soft ice-cream making.

For simplicity, the three basic attachments have been used for the majority of recipes in this book, but occasionally the plastic blade, the whipping blade, and the juice extractor have been used. If your model does not have these attachments then in all cases substitute the metal blade for the plastic blade, and follow the alternatives given for the whipping blade and juice extractor.

Here is a guide to the basic attachments and their uses together with details of the optional extras offered by many of the larger manufacturers.

Metal blade

This is probably the attachment that you will use most of all in your processor. Double-bladed and generally made of stainless steel, the blade is used to chop, purée or grind foods. This blade is especially sharp and will usually last for at least two to three years. Replacement blades are available from most stockists.

Use the metal blade to chop fresh, raw or cooked meat, fish, poultry, vegetables, nuts and fruit; to make breadcrumbs; to purée soups; to blend sauces and batters; to mix pastry and doughs and to crush ice.

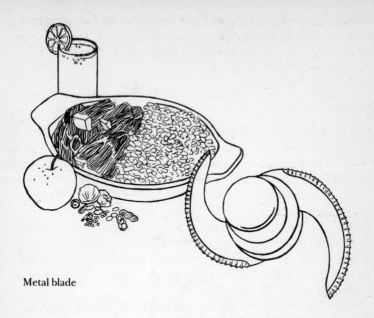

Metal blade

Plastic blade

This is the blade to use when you are mixing as opposed to chopping ingredients. It is useful for making cake mixtures and batters, creaming potatoes, mixing doughs and blending sauces.

Plastic blade

Slicing disc

Both hard and soft vegetables and fruits can be sliced through
this disc in a fraction of the time it would take by hand. Use also
to slice meats and cheese.

The effectiveness of this blade very much depends upon
cutting food to fit the feed tube and stacking it neatly within the
tube for even results. Any foods processed this way must be
pushed down the feed tube via the pusher, *never* with the
fingers.

For even slicing of long thin items like bananas, leeks, celery
or carrots it is important to stack the items upright so that they
do not fall over during processing – producing diagonal rather
than round slices.

Stacking can, therefore, also offer variety – if you prefer
crescent-shaped slices of fruit like apples and pears then
position pieces horizontally. If you prefer them to be semi-
circular then position upright. The same is true of long items
like bananas, carrots, courgettes and aubergines – slice into
circles or long strips as liked.

The basic slicing disc provided usually slices food fairly finely.
Extra attachments provide even finer or much thicker slicing
capacity.

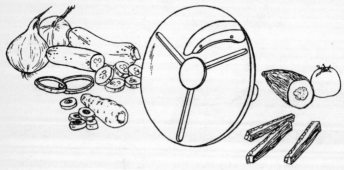

Slicing disc

Grating disc

The grating disc, designed to finely grate vegetables, fruit, cheese or chocolate, is another standard attachment available on almost every machine.

Just as in slicing, food must be cut to fit the feed tube for effective grating. Remember, however, with softer items like beetroot, semi-soft cheeses and softer cooking chocolate, not to press too hard with the pusher or items may grate to a very soft consistency.

Grating disc

Pusher

Almost every machine has a plastic pusher to process foods through the feed tube. Some manufacturers have also calibrated this item as a measuring cup for quick measuring of ingredients. Use the pusher as an aid to checking the size of food pieces before feeding through the tube to the processor.

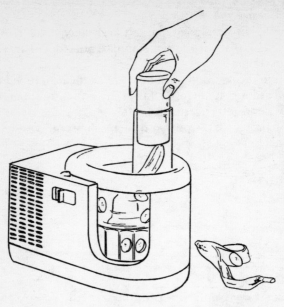

Pusher

Whipping blade

Until recently most processors on the market could not whisk egg whites or whip cream properly – only up to about 70 per cent effectiveness. This is generally due to the speed of action of the processor and its inability to introduce enough air into the food. Some manufacturers now provide a whipping blade or paddle attachment which does whip cream and whisk egg whites very effectively – made possible by incorporating holes into the blade, to introduce more air.

Such attachments can never be as effective as hand whisking since the processor has a lid which slows down the introduction of air, but they are useful in most operations. If your processor does not have this attachment then whisk by hand or with an electric beater, add to the processor and process for about two seconds to mix with other ingredients.

Whipping blade

Spatula

Almost every manufacturer supplies a plastic spatula for
scraping food down or out of the processor bowl easily. Use the
spatula during processing of foods if items build up on the
processor bowl walls.

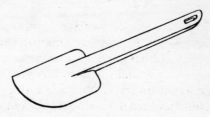

Spatula

Fine slicing or grating discs

These are optional extras that are useful in preparing vegetables
and fruits for salads and extra fine vegetables for gratin dishes.

21

Fine grating disc

Chipper or French-fry disc

A useful optional extra if your family enjoy home-made chips or French fries on a regular basis. Use it too to make julienne strips of fruits or vegetables for crudités, vegetable gratin dishes, fruit salads or dunks to serve with dips.

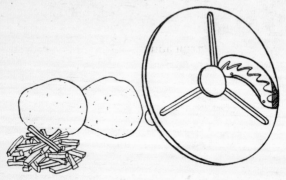

Chipper or French fry disc

Whisked sponge beater blade

Another specialist blade that is used for making cakes where the addition of air is critical for success. Use the whisked sponge beater blade for making Swiss roll and Genoese sponge cakes.

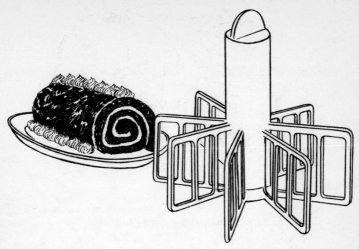

Whisked sponge beater blade

Juice extractor

Some models of food processor provide, as an optional extra, a juice extractor, making light work of extracting juice from lemons, oranges, grapefruit and limes. Many of these also have a pulp-ejecting mechanism incorporated for easy use.

Soft ice-cream maker

At the moment an extra that is only offered by one manufacturer. To make smooth, creamy ice-cream it is important to break down the ice crystals that form during freezing – and is hard work by hand, as well as being time-consuming. The soft ice-cream maker comprising a cutting disc and paddle blade makes easy work of this operation and produces smooth soft ice-cream from a solid block in just one minute. This manufacturer also supplies freezer trays for making ice cream with this attachment.

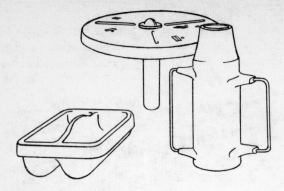

Soft ice-cream maker

Accessory storage tray or rack

An increasing number of manufacturers now supply a tray or rack for the safe storage of blades and discs. Many sit flat on a work surface while others have a wall fixing kit. If available as an optional extra, then this is a worthwhile investment since it helps to keep blades clean and sharp, and away from tiny hands.

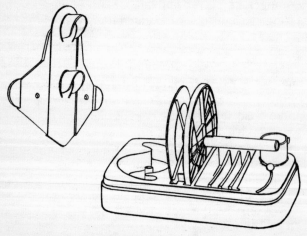

Accessory storage tray and rack

Protective covers

The chances are that you will use your processor so frequently you will hardly need a cover. Covers are, however, available for most models and do help to keep processors in pristine condition.

Golden rules before you begin

Using a food processor involves learning the basic three Rs: right order, right time and right load. Once you have mastered these golden rules you open the door to many memorable meals.

Right order

All of the recipes in this book give the ideal order for processing foods so that washing or rinsing of the processor bowl is kept to a minimum. Never assume that rinsing is necessary unless the recipe states so – only small scraps of food left from the previous process will be present and these will not interfere with the finished appearance or flavour of the dish. It is assumed, however, that effective use of the spatula provided has removed most of the food.

In general, process those foods that require a dry bowl first – items like herbs, breadcrumbs and citrus rinds. Remove from the bowl and set aside if they are to be added later in the recipe. Secondly, slice or grate any foods that need to be incorporated into chopped mixtures later. Remove and add when required. Next, process foods that require a long chopping time – items like firm vegetables and fruit. Finally, add softer foods so that uniform processing can take place, without fear of over-processing one or another of the ingredients.

For final blending or mixing add any reserved items and process for just two or three seconds for an evenly combined mixture.

Right time

The processor is one of the speediest kitchen appliances you are ever likely to use – and newcomers are often amazed by the speed with which it can chop, slice, grate, purée and mince foods. Always err on the side of safety when it comes to timing – using the pulse button if available to add a little more action if required.

Timings given in this book refer to a standard 1.8 litre (3 pint) model, not a catering or large family-size machine with an extra-powerful motor.

If you have one of the larger capacity models – up to 3.5 litres (6 pints) – you will be able to process foods in a single operation rather than in batches. Timings will also vary slightly since the motors are more powerful and therefore faster.

Remember that timings are critical – the difference between chopped and puréed vegetables being as little as two seconds. Keep your eye on the process at all times, and check frequently for best results.

Right load

Never overload your processor – it is easier and safer to process in batches if necessary.

Most of the recipes in this book have been tested on a processor with the following *ideal* load capacities:

1kg/2lb bread dough (to make and knead)
450g/1lb meat (for chopping or mincing)
575g/1¼lb shortcrust pastry (to mix)
600ml/1 pint mayonnaise (to make)
4-egg Victoria sponge (to mix)
600ml/1 pint cooked vegetables
and stock (to purée)

Processing more than the above quantities in one operation in a standard model will not save time but will simply give uneven results.

Remember to scrape down mixtures where necessary during the process for good results.

Check these foods!

Machines do vary enormously, but in general most manufacturers do not advise the processing of whole grains or coffee beans in the processor – check your handbook for guidance. Some models supply an optional attachment for crushing ice – again check this in your handbook.

Some manufacturers claim good results with whisking egg whites and whipping cream, while others do not. Some manufacturers supply attachments specially designed for these jobs – always follow your own manufacturer's instructions in this area.

Safety and care of your processor

● All parts of a processor, except the motor base are washable, and many are 'dishwasher proof'. *Never* immerse the motor base in water – simply wipe with a damp cloth to clean.

● Wash any blades, discs, pusher, lid and processor bowl in warm soapy water. Rinse and drain. The bowl is able to withstand boiling water and even melted sugar syrups – always take extra care in case of splashing when processing hot items.

● *Never* leave blades and discs soaking in dishwater. They are very sharp and can cut unsuspecting hands. Certainly keep out of reach of young children.

● Always use the plastic pusher supplied for use with the feed tube. Never use fingers, wooden spoons or other implements. The discs can easily damage fingers, while implements can irreparably damage discs and even the motor.

● Always make sure that the processor bowl or container is safely locked into position on the motor base before fitting any attachments, and before switching on.

● Never attempt to touch the blades or surrounding food until the blades have stopped revolving. Even though the lid must be in position for the blades to work it is easy to remove the lid quickly and find the blades revolving at the end of their cycle. Make a point of making sure the blades have stopped before removing the lid.

● Remove the blades, discs and attachments from the processor by a safe rounded edge or plastic centre piece – never reach in and lift out by the cutting edge.

● Never overload the machine – your manufacturer's handbook will give guidance as to maximum capacities for specific chores like dough handling, vegetable chopping and mixture puréeing. Continual overloading will put a strain on the motor or will cause interruptions in the processing by activating the overload safety cut-out.

● Always read the manufacturer's instruction booklet before use, and refer to it if in any doubt about operating the machine.

● In the unlikely event of a breakdown always contact the manufacturer or their service centre for servicing requirements. Never use a faulty machine no matter how small a problem may be.

● Look for a reputable processor with the attachments and features that ideally suit your lifestyle – checking also that the machine has BEAB or equivalent safety approval, a sensible guarantee period for machine parts and labour (twelve months minimum), and a service centre or agent if faults should occur.

Recipe guidelines

● All recipes in this book have been double-tested for success in a wide variety of food processors.

● Each has been prepared using only the three basic attachments, metal blade, grating disc and slicing disc, with optional use of the whipping blade, plastic blade and juice extractor. Use any other optional attachments you may have to speed up recipes or use with special preparation techniques.

● The recipes have been tested in both Imperial and metric measurements but the quantities are not interchangeable so only follow one set of measures.

● All spoons are level unless otherwise stated. Egg sizes are medium (sizes 3, 4) unless otherwise stated. Timings for processing, in stages, have been given as a guideline, but, since machines vary, always use your own judgement and check frequently during the processing time. In time it will become easy to adjust these timings to suit your own particular brand and model of machine.

Soups, starters and hors d'oeuvres

Creamy vichysoisse

Serves: 6
Attachments: metal blade, slicing disc

1 onion, peeled and quartered
2 large leeks, white part only, cut into pieces
3 medium potatoes, peeled and halved
15g/½oz butter
1 litre/1¾ pints light stock
salt and freshly ground white pepper
150ml/¼ pint single cream
snipped chives to garnish

Fit the metal blade. Place the onion and leeks in the processor bowl and process until chopped, about 6–8 seconds. Remove and set aside.

Fit the slicing disc. Slice the potatoes through the disc and set aside.

Melt the butter in a pan, add the onion and leek mixture and cook for 8–10 minutes. Add the potatoes, stock and salt and pepper to taste. Bring to the boil, lower the heat, and simmer for 20 minutes.

Fit the metal blade. Purée the soup in the processor bowl, in batches if necessary, about 8 seconds per batch. Return to the saucepan.

Stir in the cream, blending well, and reheat gently but do not allow to boil. Serve hot or chilled, sprinkled with snipped chives.

Chilled tomato and bean soup

Serves: 4
Attachment: metal blade

1 × 397g/14oz can tomatoes in natural juice
1 clove garlic, peeled
1 × 450g/1lb can baked beans in tomato sauce
½ cucumber, halved and seeded
1 red pepper, cored and seeded
300ml/½ pint chicken stock
4 tablespoons olive oil
salt and freshly ground black pepper

To serve:
chopped red and green peppers
onion rings
chopped cucumber
fried bread croûtons
chopped fresh parsley or snipped chives

Fit the metal blade. Place the tomatoes and their juice, garlic, beans, cucumber, red pepper, chicken stock and olive oil in the processor and blend until smooth.

Season with salt and pepper to taste and blend for 2–3 seconds to mix. If the soup is too thick for your liking, add a little extra chicken stock.

Cover and chill for 3–4 hours before serving.

Serve in small bowls accompanied by chopped peppers, onion rings, chopped cucumber and croûtons. Sprinkle with parsley or chives.

French onion soup

Serves: 4
Attachments: slicing disc, grating disc

450g/1lb onions, peeled
50g/2oz butter
1 tablespoon oil
½ teaspoon sugar
2 tablespoons plain flour
1 litre/1¾ pints rich beef stock
salt and freshly ground black pepper
100g/4oz Gruyère cheese
4 thick slices French bread
1 garlic clove, peeled and halved
2 tablespoons brandy (optional)

Fit the slicing disc. Cut the onions to fit the feed tube and slice through the disc.

Heat the butter and oil in a large heavy-based pan. Add the onions, cover and cook, over a moderate heat, for 20 minutes.

Increase the heat, stir in the sugar and cook, uncovered, stirring frequently, until the onions caramelize and turn a rich golden colour.

Add the flour and cook until golden. Gradually add the stock, blending well. Add salt and pepper to taste, bring to the boil, lower the heat, cover and simmer for 20 minutes.

Meanwhile, fit the grating disc. Grate the Gruyère through the disc.

Rub the bread slices with the cut side of the garlic clove. Place under a preheated hot grill and toast on one side. Turn over and sprinkle with the cheese. Grill until golden and bubbly.

Add the brandy to the soup, if used, and ladle into warmed soup bowls. Top with the cheese slices and serve at once.

Spicy split pea soup

Serves: 6
Attachment: metal blade

rind of 2 oranges

2 onions, peeled
225g/8oz split peas, soaked overnight in cold water
salt and freshly ground black pepper
4 tablespoons oil
½ teaspoon ground cumin
½ teaspoon ground turmeric
2 teaspoons ground coriander
juice of 2 oranges
snipped chives to garnish

Fit the metal blade. Place the orange rind in the processor bowl and process until very finely chopped, about 5 seconds. Remove and set aside.

Place the onions in the processor bowl and process until chopped, about 5 seconds. Remove and set aside.

Drain the soaking water from the peas and make up to 1.75 litres/3 pints with water. Place in a pan with soaked peas, orange rind and a good pinch of salt. Bring to the boil, lower the heat and simmer until tender, about 1 hour. Cool then purée in the processor until smooth, about 10 seconds.

Heat the oil in a large pan. Add the onion and cook until golden. Add the cumin, turmeric and coriander, blending well. Cook over a high heat for 1 minute.

Gradually add the pea purée and salt and pepper to taste. Bring to the boil, lower the heat and simmer for 10–15 minutes.

Stir in the orange juice, blending well. Adjust the seasoning if necessary and serve hot, garnished with snipped chives. Serve with chunks of wholemeal bread.

Chilled carrot and orange soup

Serves: 4
Attachments: slicing disc, metal blade, grating disc

450g/1lb carrots, peeled
rind of 1 orange
½ onion, peeled
50g/2oz butter
2 teaspoons sugar
¼ teaspoon ground ginger
¼ teaspoon ground cinnamon
2 tablespoons flour
¾ teaspoon salt
¼ teaspoon ground white pepper
750ml/1¼ pints chicken stock
400ml/14fl oz orange juice
50ml/2fl oz lemon juice

To garnish:
1 carrot, peeled
5 tablespoons cream
chopped parsley

Fit the slicing disc. Slice the carrots through the disc and set aside.

Fit the metal blade. Place the orange rind in the processor bowl and process until finely chopped, about 5 seconds. Add the onion and process for a further 4 seconds.

Melt the butter in a large pan. Add the onion and orange mixture and cook for 3 minutes. Add the carrots, sugar, ginger and cinnamon and cook for a further 3 minutes.

Blend in the flour, salt and pepper and cook for 2 minutes. Gradually add the stock and orange juice, blending well. Cover and cook for 30 minutes. Remove from the heat and allow to cool.

Add the soup to the processor bowl, in batches, and process until smooth. Stir in the lemon juice and chill thoroughly. Rinse the processor bowl.

Fit the grating disc. Grate the carrot through the disc.

Serve the soup in individual bowls topped with a little grated carrot, a swirl of cream and a sprinkling of chopped parsley.

Neufchâtel frappé

Serves: 4
Attachment: metal blade

225g/8oz Neufchâtel cheese
150ml/¼ pint natural yoghurt
150ml/¼ pint double cream
1 teaspoon orange juice
salt and freshly ground black pepper
50g/2oz broken walnuts

To serve:
shredded lettuce
tomato wedges
French toasts

Fit the metal blade. Place the cheese, yoghurt, cream, orange juice and salt and pepper to taste in the processor and process until smooth. Remove from the processor and stir in the walnuts.

Spoon into an ice cube or freezer tray and freeze until firm.

About 1½ hours before serving, remove the frappé from the freezer and leave to stand at room temperature.

To serve, scoop the frappé on to shredded lettuce and garnish with tomato wedges. Serve with French toasts.

Mushroom pâté

Serves: 4
Attachment: metal blade

1 small onion, peeled
100g/4oz butter
350g/12oz button mushrooms
1 large sprig parsley
1 clove garlic, peeled
2 teaspoons lemon juice
2 tablespoons sherry or brandy
salt and freshly ground black pepper

Fit the metal blade. Place the onion in the processor and process until coarsely chopped.

Melt half of the butter in a pan. Add the mushrooms and onion and cook for 5–7 minutes until softened.

Place the parsley and garlic in the processor and process for 5 seconds to chop. Add the mushroom and onion mixture, remaining butter, lemon juice, sherry or brandy and salt and pepper to taste. Process until smooth.

Spoon into a serving dish and chill to set. Serve with Melba toast.

Chicken quichelettes

Makes: 12
Attachment: metal blade

225g/8oz shortcrust pastry (see page 118)
rind of ½ lemon
175g/6oz cooked chicken
1 egg
150ml/¼ pint single cream
¼ teaspoon dried thyme
salt and freshly ground pepper

Fit the metal blade. Prepare the shortcrust pastry as on page 118. Roll out on a lightly-floured surface and cut out 12 rounds large enough to line 12 greased patty tins.

Place the lemon rind in the processor bowl and process until finely chopped. Add the chicken and process until chopped, about 2 seconds. Spoon evenly into the tartlet cases.

Place the egg, cream, thyme, and salt and pepper to taste in the processor and process for 3–4 seconds to blend. Pour into a jug.

Pour the cream mixture evenly over the chicken mixture and bake in a preheated moderately hot oven (190°C, 375°F, gas mark 5) for about 25 minutes until golden and set. Serve warm or cold.

Hummous

Serves: 4
Attachment: metal blade

1 × 425g/15oz can chick peas, drained
1 small onion, peeled and quartered
1 clove garlic, peeled
150ml/¼ pint natural yoghurt
2 teaspoons lemon juice
pinch of ground cumin
salt and freshly ground black pepper
pitta bread to serve

Fit the metal blade. Place the chick peas, onion and garlic in the processor bowl and process until smooth, about 8 seconds.

Scrape down the bowl and add the yoghurt, lemon juice, cumin and salt and pepper to taste. Process for 10 seconds until well mixed. Chill thoroughly.

Serve with warm pitta bread.

Smoked mackerel pâté

Serves: 4
Attachment: metal blade

50g/2oz unsalted butter, diced
225g/8oz smoked mackerel fillets, skinned
2 tablespoons mayonnaise
2 tablespoons soured cream
¾–1 teaspoon garlic purée
freshly ground black pepper
toasted brown bread fingers to serve

Fit the metal blade. Place the butter and mackerel in the processor bowl and process for 20 seconds.

Add the mayonnaise, soured cream, garlic purée and pepper to taste. Process until smooth, about 5–8 seconds.

Spoon the pâté into 4 ramekin dishes, level the tops and chill until firm. Serve lightly chilled with hot toasted brown bread fingers.

Note: The processor can help you to make garlic purée in bulk for recipes. Peel about 20 cloves of garlic and place in the processor bowl with a pinch of salt. Process until smooth or finely chopped, about 20 seconds, scraping down about half way through the time. Add 2 tablespoons of oil and process for a further 5 seconds. Place in a screw-topped jar and cover with a little more oil. Store in the refrigerator for up to 2 months.

Spicy Indian kebab with cucumber and mint dressing

Serves: 6
Attachments: grating disc, metal blade

1 small onion, peeled
675g/1½lb chuck steak, cubed
2 cloves garlic, peeled
1 tablespoon flour
½ teaspoon chilli powder
½ teaspoon ground cumin
½ teaspoon ground coriander
pinch of ground ginger
pinch of ground cinnamon
pinch of ground cloves
juice of ½ lemon
1 tablespoon tomato purée
salt and freshly ground black pepper

Dressing:
4 sprigs fresh mint
¼ cucumber
4 tablespoons mayonnaise
2 tablespoons natural yoghurt
shredded lettuce to serve
lemon slices to garnish

Fit the grating disc. Cut the onion to fit the feed tube and grate through the disc. Remove and set aside.

Fit the metal blade. Place the beef and garlic in the processor bowl and process for 8 seconds to mince. Add the onion, flour, spices, lemon juice, tomato purée and salt and pepper to taste. Process for 5 seconds to blend.

Divide the mixture into 6 equal portions, shape each into a long sausage shape and thread on to a wooden skewer. Chill to firm, about 30 minutes. Rinse the processor bowl.

Fit the metal blade. Place the mint in the processor bowl and process until finely chopped, about 5 seconds. Add the cucumber and process for 2 seconds to chop. Add the mayonnaise and yoghurt and process for 1 second to blend.

Cook the kebabs under a preheated moderate grill for about 15–20 minutes, turning occasionally.

Serve the kebabs on a bed of shredded lettuce. Spoon over equal quantities of the cucumber and mint dressing and garnish with lemon slices.

Cut and come again pâté

Serves: 6–8
Attachment: metal blade

6 rashers streaky bacon, rinded
1 large onion, peeled and quartered
1 clove garlic, peeled
75g/3oz butter
225g/8oz sliced pig's liver
225g/8oz fat bacon, cubed
25g/1oz flour
150ml/¼ pint milk
150ml/¼ pint dry cider, apple juice or red wine
salt and freshly ground black pepper
bay leaves
5 tablespoons liquid aspic

Stretch the bacon with the back of a knife and use to line the base and sides of a greased 450g/1lb terrine.

Fit the metal blade. Place the onion and garlic in the processor bowl and process until chopped, about 4 seconds.

Melt 50g/2oz of the butter in a large pan. Add the liver, fat bacon, onion and garlic mixture and cook, over a moderate heat, for 10 minutes.

Spoon the mixture into the processor bowl and process until smooth, about 15 seconds.

Meanwhile, melt the remaining butter in a pan. Add the flour and cook for 1 minute. Gradually add the milk and cider, apple juice or red wine, blending well. Bring to the boil and cook for 3 minutes. Season with salt and pepper to taste. Add to the liver mixture and process for 4 seconds to blend.

Spoon into the terrine and level the top. Top with the bay leaves and buttered foil. Place in a roasting pan half-full of water. Cook in a preheated moderate oven (180°C, 350°F, gas mark 4) for about 1 hour or until just firm to the touch. Allow to cool.

Pour the aspic over the pâté to keep it moist and chill thoroughly. Slice to serve.

Cheese and chicken nutties

Makes: about 24
Attachments: metal blade, plastic blade

100g/4oz salted peanuts
100g/4oz cooked chicken, skinned
2 spring onions, trimmed
225g/8oz cream cheese
freshly ground black pepper

Fit the metal blade. Place the nuts in the processor and process until coarsely chopped. Remove and set aside.

Add the chicken and spring onions to the processor and process until finely chopped.

Fit the plastic blade. Add the cream cheese to the chicken and onion mixture and process until well blended.

Form into small balls about the size of walnuts and coat in the chopped nuts. Chill until required.

Serve on cocktail sticks.

Crispy chicken puffs

Makes: about 24
Attachment: metal blade

4 tablespoons plain flour

1 egg
150ml/¼ pint water
pinch of ground mace
1 teaspoon baking powder
salt and freshly ground pepper
350g/12oz cooked chicken, cut into bite-sized pieces
oil for deep frying

Fit the metal blade. Place the flour, egg, water, mace, baking powder, and salt and pepper to taste in the processor and process for 10 seconds to make a smooth batter.

Coat the chicken pieces in the batter and deep fry in hot oil until puffed and golden brown, about 4–5 minutes. Drain on absorbent kitchen towel.

Serve hot with a sweet and sour or spicy tomato sauce.

Creamy chicken dip

Makes: about 300ml/½ pint
Attachment: metal blade

100g/4oz cooked chicken, skinned
1 clove garlic, peeled
150ml/¼ pint mayonnaise
2 tablespoons tomato purée
salt and freshly ground black pepper

Fit the metal blade. Place the chicken and garlic in the processor and process until very finely chopped.

Add the mayonnaise, tomato purée and salt and pepper to taste. Process until well blended.

Serve chilled with a selection of savoury biscuits and raw vegetables – crudité style.

Minted ratatouille

Serves: 4
Attachments: slicing disc, metal blade

225g/8oz aubergine
225g/8oz courgettes
225g/8oz onions, peeled
100g/4oz mushrooms
1 green pepper, cored and seeded
1 small bunch fresh mint
1 clove garlic, peeled
450g/1lb ripe tomatoes, seeded
4 tablespoons oil
salt and freshly ground black pepper
grated Parmesan cheese to serve

Fit the slicing disc. Cut the aubergine, courgettes, onions, mushrooms and pepper to fit the feed tube and slice through the disc. Remove and set aside.

Fit the metal blade. Place the mint and garlic in the processor bowl and process until finely chopped. Remove and set aside. Add the tomatoes to the processor bowl and process to chop, about 2 seconds.

Heat the oil in a pan. Add the onion mixture and sauté for 5 minutes.

Add the mint and garlic, tomatoes and salt and pepper to taste, blending well. Cover and cook for 30–45 minutes until very tender, stirring occasionally.

Serve hot or cold, sprinkled with Parmesan cheese.

Quick meals and snacks

St Paulin stuffed spinach

Serves: 4–6
Attachment: metal blade

450g/1lb fresh spinach leaves (about 30), washed
225g/8oz St Paulin cheese, cut into small cubes
ground nutmeg
1 × 227g/8oz can tomatoes
1 teaspoon tomato pureé
½ clove garlic, peeled
salt and freshly ground black pepper
French bread to serve

Cook the spinach leaves in boiling salted water for ½ minute, drain and cool. Spread some of the leaves out flat on a board, place a cube of cheese in the centre of each and sprinkle with a little nutmeg.

Carefully wrap up each cube of cheese in a spinach leaf, folding in the edges, and place in a shallow ovenproof dish with joins underneath, packing the spinach rolls closely together.

Fit the metal blade. Place the tomatoes and their juice, tomato purée, garlic and salt and pepper to taste in the processor and blend until smooth. Transfer to a saucepan and bring to the boil. Pour over the spinach parcels.

Cover and cook in the centre of a moderately hot oven (200°C, 400°F, gas mark 6) for 15–20 minutes. Serve at once with French bread.

Pizza Napoletana

Serves: 4–6
Attachments: plastic blade, metal blade, slicing disc, grating disc

Bread base:
1 teaspoon sugar
200ml/7fl oz warm water
1½ teaspoons dried active yeast
350g/12oz plain flour
1 teaspoon salt
25g/1oz butter

Topping:
225g/8oz tomatoes, peeled and seeded
3 tablespoons tomato purée
½ teaspoon dried basil
½ teaspoon dried oregano
1 onion, peeled and halved
1 green pepper, cored, seeded and halved
50g/2oz button mushrooms
salt and freshly ground black pepper
1 × 50g/1¾oz can anchovy fillets, drained
few black olives
100g/4oz Mozzarella cheese

Dissolve the sugar in the water. Sprinkle the yeast on top and leave to stand until well-risen and frothy, about 15 minutes.

Fit the plastic blade, place the flour, salt and butter in the processor and process until well mixed. Add the yeast mixture through the feed tube with the motor running and process until the dough is well blended and lightly kneaded, about 1 minute. This process can also be done with a dough blade or hook if your processor has this special attachment.

Turn the dough on to a lightly-floured surface and shape into a round. Place in an oiled plastic bag and leave in a warm place until doubled in size, about 40 minutes.

Turn on to a lightly-floured surface and roll out to a 25cm/10in round. Place on an oiled baking sheet.

Fit the metal blade and place the tomatoes, tomato purée and herbs in the processor bowl. Process until puréed, about 5 seconds. Spread over the pizza base and remove and wash the processor bowl.

Fit the slicing disc. Slice the onion, pepper and mushrooms through the disc and remove. Arrange over the tomato topping and season with salt and pepper to taste.

Arrange a lattice of anchovy fillets and olives over the vegetables.

Fit the grating disc and grate the cheese. Sprinkle over the pizza and bake in a preheated moderately hot oven (190°C, 375°F, gas mark 5) for 25–35 minutes or until the base is cooked and the top is golden and bubbly.

Creamy courgette flan

Serves: 4–6
Attachments: grating disc, metal blade, slicing disc, plastic blade

Pastry:
75g/3oz Cheddar cheese
175g/6oz plain flour
1 teaspoon dried mixed herbs
1 tablespoon chopped parsley
½ teaspoon salt
75g/3oz butter, diced
3 tablespoons water

Filling:
450g/1lb courgettes
300ml/½ pint single cream
3 eggs
salt and freshly ground black pepper
1–2 teaspoons lightly-crushed mustard seeds

Fit the grating disc. Grate the cheese and set aside. Fit the metal blade. Place the flour, dried herbs, parsley, salt and butter in the processor bowl and process for 7–8 seconds or until the mixture resembles fine breadcrumbs. Add the cheese and process for 2 seconds to mix. Add the water, a tablespoon at a time, through the feed tube with the motor running and process until the ingredients just bind together to make a ball. Turn on to a lightly-floured surface and knead lightly until smooth and free from cracks. Wrap in polythene or cling film and chill for 15 minutes.

Fit the slicing disc. Slice the courgettes through the disc and set aside. Fit the plastic blade. Place the cream, eggs and salt and pepper to taste in the processor bowl and process until smooth, about 5 seconds.

Roll out the pastry and use to line a greased 25cm/10in flan tin. Arrange the courgettes in the flan and pour over the cream mixture. Sprinkle with the crushed mustard seeds.

Bake in a preheated moderately hot oven (190°C, 375°F, gas mark 5) for 35–40 minutes until golden and just set. Serve hot, warm or cold.

Stuffed gammon steaks

Serves: 4
Attachment: metal blade

rind of ½ orange
100g/4oz fresh white bread, cubed
1 banana, peeled
50g/2oz almonds, halved and toasted
juice of ½ orange
salt and freshly ground black pepper
4 gammon steaks

Fit the metal blade. Place the orange rind in the processor bowl and process until finely chopped, about 3 seconds. Add the bread, through the feed tube, with the motor running, to make breadcrumbs. Remove and set aside.

Place the banana in the processor bowl and process for 1 second until very coarsely chopped. Add the almonds, orange juice, breadcrumb mixture and salt and pepper to taste. Process for a further 2 seconds to mix.

Cut the rind from the gammon steaks and snip the fat at intervals to avoid the edges curling. Spread the banana mixture evenly over the gammon steaks. Fold the gammon over to enclose the stuffing, securing with wooden cocktail sticks or metal skewers. Place in an ovenproof dish.

Bake in a preheated moderately hot oven (200°C, 400°F, gas mark 6) for 35–45 minutes. Serve hot.

St Paulin rolls

Serves: 4
Attachment: metal blade

1 small onion, peeled
2 sticks celery, trimmed
50g/2oz mushrooms
1 sprig parsley
25g/1oz butter
pinch of dried sage
150ml/¼ pint natural yoghurt
dash of Worcestershire sauce
salt and freshly ground black pepper
8 slices cooked ham
225g/8oz St Paulin cheese, sliced

To garnish:
parsley sprigs
tomato wedges

Fit the metal blade. Place the onion, celery, mushrooms and parsley in the processor bowl and process until chopped, about 4 seconds.

Melt the butter in a pan. Add the onion mixture and cook until softened, about 5 minutes. Remove from the heat and add the sage, 1 tablespoon of the yoghurt, Worcestershire sauce and salt and pepper to taste.

To assemble the rolls, cover each slice of ham with 2 slices of the cheese. Place 2 teaspoons of the stuffing along the centre and roll to enclose. Secure with a wooden cocktail stick if necessary.

Place in a shallow ovenproof dish, cover with lightly greased foil and bake in a preheated moderately hot oven (190°C, 375°F, gas mark 5) for 15 minutes.

Remove the foil, top with the remaining yoghurt and bake for a further 5 minutes. Serve hot, garnished with parsley sprigs and tomato wedges.

Sausagemeat grills

Serves: 4–6
Attachment: metal blade

2 sprigs parsley
2–3 pickled onions
450g/1lb pork sausagemeat
4–6 tablespoons coarse oatmeal

Fit the metal blade. Place the parsley and pickled onions in the processor bowl and process until finely chopped.

Add the sausagemeat and process to blend, about 3 seconds.

Divide into six portions and shape each into a flat patty. Coat with the oatmeal, pressing on well.

Cook under a preheated hot grill for 20 minutes, turning every 5 minutes. Serve hot with a salad.

Hamburgers with pizzaiola sauce

Serves: 4
Attachments: metal blade, slicing disc

Hamburgers:
450g/1lb chuck steak, cubed
pinch of dry mustard powder
salt and freshly ground black pepper

Sauce:
2 medium onions, peeled
2 cloves garlic, peeled
2 green peppers, cored and seeded
50g/2oz mushrooms
2 teaspoons oil
1 × 397g/14oz can tomatoes
2 teaspoons dried oregano or marjoram
dash of hot chilli sauce
salt and pepper

Fit the metal blade. Place the chuck steak, mustard and salt and pepper to taste in the processor bowl and process for 5–6 seconds until the meat is minced. Divide into 4 portions and shape each into a hamburger, taking care not to overhandle and compress the beef too much.

Place the onions and garlic in the processor bowl and process until chopped. Remove and set aside.

Fit the slicing disc. Slice the peppers and mushrooms through the disc.

Heat the oil in a pan. Add the onion and garlic mixture and cook until golden. Add the pepper and mushroom mixture and cook, stirring often, for 15 minutes. Add the tomatoes with their juice, dried herbs, chilli sauce, and salt and pepper to taste. Cover and cook for a further 10–15 minutes.

Meanwhile, grill the hamburgers under a preheated hot grill for 3 minutes, each side. Arrange on a warmed serving dish and spoon over the pizzaiola sauce. Serve with a green salad.

Cornish pasties

Makes: 4
Attachment: metal blade

225g/8oz shortcrust pastry (see page 118)
1 onion, peeled and quartered
2 medium potatoes, peeled and halved
1 carrot, peeled and halved
2 sprigs fresh parsley
225g/8oz lean beef steak, cubed
salt and freshly ground black pepper
2 tablespoons beef stock
beaten egg to glaze

Fit the metal blade. Make the pastry as on page 118. Chill until required.

Place the onion in the processor bowl and process for 3–4 seconds until chopped. Remove and set aside.

Place the potatoes and carrot in the processor and process for 5 seconds to chop. Remove and set aside.

With the motor running, add the parsley through the feed

tube and process for 3 seconds. Add the meat, onion, potato and carrot mixture, salt and pepper to taste and stock. Process for 2–3 seconds to mix.

Roll out the prepared pastry on a lightly-floured surface and cut out 4 × 20 cm/8in rounds. Divide the meat and vegetable mixture between the rounds. Dampen the pastry edges with water and draw together to make a seam across the top. Crimp the edges decoratively.

Place on a greased baking tray and brush with beaten egg to glaze. Cook in a preheated hot oven (220°C, 425°F, gas mark 7) for 15 minutes. Reduce the oven temperature to moderate (160°C, 325°F, gas mark 3) and cook for a further 50 minutes.

Nut and cinnamon lamb balls

Serves: 6
Attachment: metal blade

4 sprigs fresh parsley
1 small onion, peeled and quartered
450g/1lb lean lamb, cubed
1 tablespoon raisins, soaked in a little water then drained
2 tablespoons broken walnuts
1 teaspoon ground allspice
½ teaspoon ground cinnamon
salt and freshly ground black pepper
1 egg
oil for cooking

Fit the metal blade. Place the parsley in the processor bowl and process until finely chopped. Remove and set aside.

Place the onion in the processor bowl and process until coarsely chopped, about 3 seconds. Add the lamb and process until minced, about 8 seconds.

Add the parsley, raisins, walnuts, allspice, cinnamon, salt and pepper to taste, and the egg. Process until well mixed, about 6–8 seconds.

Divide the mixture into about 18 small balls and fry in oil, turning frequently, until browned and cooked through, about 15–20 minutes. Drain on absorbent kitchen towel.

Serve hot with vegetables in season or cold with a seasonal salad.

Tagliatelle with pesto sauce

Serves: 4
Attachment: metal blade

350g/12oz tagliatelle
25g/1oz fresh basil leaves
2 cloves garlic, peeled
50g/2oz pine kernels
50g/2oz Parmesan cheese
75ml/3fl oz olive oil
salt and freshly ground black pepper

Cook the tagliatelle in boiling salted water according to the packet instructions.

Meanwhile, fit the metal blade. Place the basil, garlic and pine kernels in the processor bowl and process until very finely chopped, about 10 seconds. Add the Parmesan cheese and process for a further 10 seconds, scraping the bowl down half-way through the processing time.

With the motor running, add the oil in a steady stream through the feed tube and process to make a thick sauce, about 6–8 seconds.

Drain the cooked tagliatelle and place in a warmed serving dish. Top with the pesto sauce and toss lightly to blend. Serve at once.

Family main meals and desserts

Mexican meatballs

Serves: 4
Attachment: metal blade

Meatballs:
450g/1lb braising steak, cubed
1 medium onion, peeled and quartered
2 cloves garlic, peeled
1 tablespoon Worcestershire sauce
2 teaspoons chilli powder
1 egg
salt and freshly ground black pepper

2 tablespoons flour
2 tablespoons oil for frying

Sauce:
1 × 220g/7.75oz can pimentos, drained
350g/12oz tomatoes, peeled and seeded
2 tablespoons tomato purée
150ml/¼ pint hot beef stock
¼ teaspoon ground bayleaves
salt and pepper

Fit the metal blade. Place the steak in the processor and process until minced, about 4–6 seconds.

Add the onion, garlic, Worcestershire sauce, chilli powder, egg and salt and pepper to taste. Process for a further 4–6 seconds until blended. Remove the mixture and shape into 16 small meatballs and coat each in a little flour.

Heat the oil in a deep frying pan. Add the meatballs and fry until browned on all sides.

Meanwhile place the pimentos, tomatoes, tomato purée, beef stock, ground bayleaves and salt and pepper to taste in the processor bowl and process until smooth and puréed, about 8–10 seconds. Pour the sauce over the meatballs and stir well to blend.

Cover and cook, over a moderate heat, for about 15 minutes or until the meatballs are cooked and the sauce is thickened.

Adjust the seasoning then serve with boiled rice and corn chips.

Chinese beef stir-fry

Serves: 4
Attachments: metal blade, slicing disc

2 cloves garlic, peeled
1 × 2.5cm/1in piece fresh root ginger, peeled
1 onion, peeled and halved
1 small green pepper, cored, seeded and halved
1 small red pepper, cored, seeded and halved
1 small courgette, topped and tailed
100g/4oz button mushrooms
1½ teaspoons cornflour
4 tablespoons soy sauce
2 tablespoons sherry
2–3 tablespoons oil
450g/1lb rump steak, cut into thin strips
1 teaspoon Chinese 5-spice powder
salt

Fit the metal blade. Place the garlic and ginger in the processor bowl and process until finely chopped.

Fit the slicing disc. Slice the onion, green pepper, red pepper, courgette and mushrooms through the disc.

Blend the cornflour with the soy sauce and sherry until well mixed.

Heat the oil in a large frying pan or wok until very hot. Add the beef and stir-fry for 2 minutes. Add the Chinese 5-spice powder and prepared vegetables and stir-fry for 1–2 minutes until softened but still crisp.

Stir in the cornflour mixture and cook until the juices are thickened. Season with salt to taste and serve at once.

Quick bean cassoulet

Serves: 6
Attachments: metal blade, slicing disc

4 sprigs fresh thyme
2 cloves garlic, peeled
1 thick slice smoked bacon, weighing about 175g/6oz, rinded

1 leek, trimmed
1 large carrot, peeled
1 small onion, peeled and halved
350g/12oz pork fillet, cubed
freshly ground black pepper
450ml/¾ pint chicken stock
12 rashers streaky bacon, rinded
2 × 450g/1lb cans baked beans in tomato sauce
175g/6oz sliced garlic sausage
4 tomatoes, skinned and seeded
4 tablespoons dried breadcrumbs

Fit the metal blade. Place the thyme and garlic in the processor bowl and process until finely chopped. Remove and add the bacon and process until coarsely chopped. Remove and fit the slicing disc. Slice the leek, carrot and onion through the disc.

Place the bacon, pork fillet, leek, carrot, onion and half of the garlic and thyme mixture in a pan. Add pepper to taste and the stock. Bring to the boil, lower the heat and simmer until the meats are tender, about 20 minutes. Drain, reserving the stock.

Line the base and sides of an earthenware casserole with two-thirds of the bacon rashers. Mix the beans with the remaining garlic and thyme mixture and garlic sausage. Spoon half of the bean mixture into the casserole and top with the meat and vegetable mixture.

Fit the metal blade. Add the tomatoes to the processor bowl and process until coarsely chopped. Spoon on top of the meat and vegetable mixture. Add the remaining beans and spoon over 4 tablespoons of the reserved cooking liquor. Top with the remaining bacon rashers.

Cover and cook in a preheated moderate oven (180°C, 350°F, gas mark 4) for 45 minutes. Remove the lid, sprinkle with the breadcrumbs and cook, uncovered, for a further 15 minutes. Serve hot.

Lemon and herb marinated lamb chops

Serves: 4
Attachment: metal blade

rind of 1 lemon
3 sprigs parsley
1 clove garlic, peeled
1 bay leaf
4 tablespoons olive oil
juice of 1 lemon
pinch of dried sage
pinch of dried oregano
salt and freshly ground black pepper
8 small lamb loin chops

Fit the metal blade. Place the lemon rind, parsley, garlic and bay leaf in the processor and process until finely chopped, about 5–8 seconds. Add the oil, lemon juice, sage, oregano and salt and pepper to taste. Process for 2 seconds to mix.

Place the chops in a shallow dish and pour over the lemon and herb marinade. Leave to marinate for 4–5 hours.

Remove the chops from the marinade with a slotted spoon and either cook under a preheated hot grill for 10 minutes each side or bake in a preheated moderately hot oven (200°C, 400°F, gas mark 6) for about 45 minutes. Baste the chops frequently with the marinade during cooking. Serve with sautéed new potatoes and a seasonal salad.

Turkey croquettes

Serves: 4
Attachment: metal blade

75g/3oz stale or day-old white bread, cubed
350g/12oz cooked turkey meat
25g/1oz butter
3 tablespoons plain flour
300ml/½ pint milk
salt and freshly ground black pepper
3 tablespoons tarragon and thyme mustard

1 egg, beaten
oil for deep frying

Fit the metal blade. Add the bread cubes through the feed tube, with the motor running, to make fine dry breadcrumbs. Remove and place in a shallow dish.

Add the turkey meat and process to chop finely, about 3–5 seconds.

Meanwhile, melt the butter in a pan. Add the flour, and cook for 1 minute. Gradually add the milk, bring to the boil and cook for 2–3 minutes, stirring constantly. Season to taste with salt and pepper.

Add with the mustard to the turkey in the processor. Process for 2–3 seconds to blend. Chill the mixture until firm.

Divide the mixture into eight portions and shape each into a finger croquette. Dip in the beaten egg then roll in the breadcrumbs. Deep fry in hot oil until golden and cooked through, about 10 minutes.

Drain on absorbent kitchen towel and serve with a salad.

Fruity pork pasties

Makes: 6
Attachment: metal blade

350g/12oz wholemeal pastry (see page 119)
450g/1lb boneless pork, cubed
2 sprigs parsley
1 onion, peeled and quartered
2 teaspoons wholegrain mustard
salt and freshly ground black pepper
75g/3oz cranberry sauce
beaten egg to glaze

Fit the metal blade. Prepare the pastry as on page 119. Chill for 15 minutes.

Place the pork in the processor bowl and process for 7–8 seconds to mince. Remove and set aside.

Place the parsley in the processor bowl and process until finely chopped. Add the onion and process further until finely chopped, about 4 seconds.

Add the pork, mustard and salt and pepper to taste. Process to blend, about 4 seconds. Divide into 6 portions and shape each into a flat patty.

Roll out the pastry on a lightly-floured surface and cut out 12 rounds, slightly larger than the patties. Place a patty on six of the pastry rounds. Top each patty with a spoonful of the cranberry sauce. Brush the pastry edges with beaten egg, top with the remaining pastry rounds and pinch to seal the edges.

Place on a greased baking tray and glaze with beaten egg. Bake in a preheated moderately hot oven (200°C, 400°F, gas mark 6) for 45 minutes until cooked and golden brown. Serve hot or cold.

Grilled mackerel with rhubarb sauce

Serves: 4
Attachment: metal blade

4 mackerel
salt and freshly ground black pepper
1 tablespoon oil

Sauce:
225g/8oz rhubarb, trimmed and chopped
3 tablespoons clear honey
4 tablespoons water
15g/½oz butter
watercress or parsley sprigs to garnish

Prepare the fish by removing the heads and fins. Make a slit along the belly cavity and remove the insides, scraping away any black skin. Wash under cold running water and dry on absorbent kitchen towel.

Remove the backbone if preferred by placing the fish, skin-side up, on a work surface and, using your thumb, pressing along the backbone to loosen it. Turn the fish over and ease away the bone, freeing it at the tail. Remove as many other small bones as possible. Season with salt and pepper to taste, and brush with the oil.

Either fold the fish back to their original shape and make 3 diagonal slashes on each side, or leave flat.

Grill, under medium heat, for 6–8 minutes for an opened-out fish, or 15–20 minutes for a whole fish, turning once.

Meanwhile, fit the metal blade. Make the sauce by placing the rhubarb, honey and water in a pan. Bring to the boil then simmer gently for 10–12 minutes. Place in the processor with the butter and blend until smooth.

Arrange the fish on a warmed serving dish and spoon over the rhubarb sauce. Garnish with watercress or parsley sprigs.

Bramley scalloped fish

Serves: 4–5
Attachments: metal blade, slicing disc

675g/1½lb skinned white fish fillets (cod or haddock for example)
300ml/½ pint milk
2 bay leaves
1 tablespoon lemon juice
salt and freshly ground white pepper
1 small onion, peeled
100g/4oz mushrooms
225g/8oz Bramley or other cooking apples
40g/1½oz butter
25g/1oz flour
2–3 tablespoons cream
900g/2lb potatoes, peeled
milk

To garnish:
few slices apple
parsley sprigs

Poach the fish in the milk with the bay leaves, lemon juice and salt and pepper to taste, for about 10 minutes. Drain off the cooking liquor and make up to 300ml/½ pint again with water or milk. Discard the bay leaves and flake the fish.

Fit the metal blade. Place the onion in the processor bowl and process until chopped. Remove and add the mushrooms. Process until chopped. Remove and fit the slicing disc. Peel and core the apples and slice through the disc.

Melt the butter in a pan. Add the onion and cook for 2–3

minutes. Add the mushrooms and cook for a further 2–3 minutes. Stir in the flour and cook for 1 minute. Gradually add the cooking liquor and bring to the boil. Add the apples and cook for 2 minutes. Stir in the cream and flaked fish, blending well. Turn into a shallow ovenproof dish.

Cook the potatoes in boiling salted water until tender, about 25 minutes. Drain and place in the processor. Process for about 5 seconds until smooth. Add sufficient milk to give a stiff piping consistency to the potato.

Pipe or spoon the potato attractively on top of the fish and apple mixture. Cook in a preheated moderately hot oven (200°C, 400°F, gas mark 6) for 30 minutes until tinged golden. Serve garnished with slices of apple and parsley sprigs.

Bobotie

Serves: 4
Attachment: metal blade

675g/1½lb chuck steak, cubed
2 onions, peeled
1 cooking apple, peeled, cored and quartered
1 tablespoon oil
1 tablespoon mild curry powder
50g/2oz raisins
50g/2oz peanuts
juice of 1 small lemon
salt and freshly ground black pepper
2 bay leaves
2 eggs
200ml/7fl oz milk

Fit the metal blade. Place the steak in the processor and process until minced, about 5–7 seconds. Remove and set aside.

Place the onions in the processor bowl and process until chopped, about 5 seconds. Remove and set aside.

Place the apple in the processor bowl and process until chopped, about 4 seconds.

Heat the oil in a large pan. Add the onion and sauté for 3 minutes. Add the beef and apple and sauté, stirring constantly, for 3 minutes.

Add the curry powder and cook for 1 minute. Stir in the raisins, peanuts and lemon juice, blending well. Add salt and pepper to taste and cook, over a low heat, for 5 minutes.

Transfer the mixture to a 1-litre/1¾ pint ovenproof dish. Press the bay leaves into the top, cover with foil and bake in a preheated moderate oven (180°C, 350°F, gas mark 4) for 45 minutes.

Meanwhile, beat the egg with the milk and seasoning to taste. Pour over the meat mixture, discarding the bay leaves. Return to the oven and bake for a further 15–20 minutes or until the topping has set. Serve hot with a salad.

Pork and bacon meatloaf

Serves: 6–8
Attachment: metal blade

100g/4oz fresh white bread, cubed
1 onion, peeled and quartered
450g/1lb belly of pork, cubed
225g/8oz unsmoked back bacon, rinded
1 teaspoon mustard powder
½ teaspoon dried mixed herbs
1 egg
150ml/¼ pint cider

Fit the metal blade. Add the bread cubes through the feed tube, with the motor running, to make breadcrumbs. Remove and set aside.

Place the onion in the processor bowl and process until finely chopped, about 5 seconds. Remove and set aside.

Place the pork and bacon in the processor bowl and process until minced, about 8–10 seconds. Add the breadcrumbs, onion, mustard powder, herbs, egg and cider. Process to blend well, about 5–7 seconds.

Spoon into a greased 900g/2lb loaf tin, pressing down firmly. Cover with foil and bake in a preheated moderate oven (180°C, 350°F, gas mark 4) for about 1½ hours.

Remove from the tin and allow to cool. Serve cold sliced with salad and boiled potatoes.

Breast of lamb with grapefruit stuffing

Serves: 6
Attachment: metal blade

rind of 2 grapefruit
4 sprigs fresh parsley
6 sprigs fresh mint
225g/8oz fresh white bread, cubed
1 large onion, peeled and quartered
75g/3oz butter
flesh of 2 grapefruit
1 egg
salt and freshly ground black pepper
2 breasts of lamb, weighing about 675g/1½lb each
grapefruit segments and mint sprigs to garnish

Fit the metal blade. Place the grapefruit rind in the processor bowl and process until finely chopped, about 5–8 seconds. Remove and set aside.

Place the parsley and mint in the processor bowl and process until finely chopped, about 5 seconds. Remove and set aside.

Add the bread cubes through the feed tube, with the motor running, to make breadcrumbs. Remove and set aside.

Place the onion in the processor and process until chopped, about 5 seconds.

Melt 50g/2oz of the butter in a pan and add the onion. Cook, over a gentle heat for 5 minutes. Return to the processor bowl with the grapefruit rind, herbs, breadcrumbs, grapefruit flesh, egg and salt and pepper to taste. Process until well combined, about 5 seconds.

Place one lamb breast flat on a board and cover with the grapefruit stuffing. Top with the second breast of lamb and secure together with string at about 5cm/2in intervals.

Place in a baking dish, season with salt and pepper and dot with the remaining butter. Cook in a preheated moderate oven (180°C, 350°F, gas mark 4) for 1 hour.

Increase the oven temperature to moderately hot (200°C, 400°F, gas mark 6) and cook for a further 20 minutes.

Remove and discard the string and serve at once garnished with grapefruit segments and sprigs of mint. Cut into slices to serve.

Herby whiting roll-ups

Serves: 4
Attachment: metal blade

4 sprigs fresh tarragon
50g/2oz fresh white bread, cubed
rind of 1 lemon
juice of 1 lemon
25g/1oz raisins
4 large whiting fillets, skinned
mushroom and lemon sauce (see page 86)
parsley or tarragon sprigs to garnish

Fit the metal blade. Place the tarragon in the processor bowl and process until finely chopped, about 4 seconds.

With the motor running, add the bread cubes through the feed tube and process to make crumbs. Remove the herby breadcrumbs and set aside.

Place the lemon rind in the processor bowl and process until finely chopped, about 5 seconds. Add the herby breadcrumbs, lemon juice and raisins and process for 3–4 seconds until evenly mixed.

Spread equal amounts of the stuffing on the fillets of whiting, and roll up. Secure with wooden cocktail sticks if liked. Place in a shallow ovenproof dish.

Prepare the mushroom and lemon sauce as on page 86 and spoon over the fish. Cover and bake in a preheated moderate oven (180°C, 350°F, gas mark 4) for 35–40 minutes or until the fish is cooked. Serve garnished with parsley or tarragon sprigs.

Tropical chocolate cups

Makes: 6
Attachment: plastic blade

100g/4oz plain chocolate
10 tablespoons lime curd
2 tablespoons natural yoghurt
6 tablespoons double cream

Melt the chocolate in a bowl over a saucepan of hot water. Use the melted chocolate to coat the insides of six paper baking cases, then turn the cases upside down so that the chocolate edges remain thicker than the base. Chill until set. When well chilled, carefully peel off the paper cases.

Fit the plastic blade. Place 8 tablespoons of the lime curd and yoghurt in the processor and process until well blended.

Pour the cream in through the feed tube, with the motor running, and process for 5–6 seconds until thick. Spoon into the chocolate cups.

Place in freezer until half-frozen then spoon a little of the remaining lime curd on top of each and, with a skewer, swirl for a decorative effect. Serve at once.

Pudding pancakes with lemon sauce

Makes: 14
Attachments: metal blade, plastic blade

Pancakes:
100g/4oz self-raising flour
2 eggs
pinch of salt
300ml/½ pint milk
1 tablespoon lemon juice
1 tablespoon caster sugar
50g/2oz shelled walnuts
50g/2oz crystallized ginger
100g/4oz chopped mixed peel
oil for frying

Sauce:
150ml/¼ pint natural yoghurt
150ml/¼ pint soured cream
2 tablespoons lemon juice
1 tablespoon caster sugar

Fit the metal blade. Place the flour, eggs, salt, milk, lemon juice and sugar in the processor and process for 10 seconds to make a smooth batter. Remove and wash processor bowl.

Fit the metal blade. Place the walnuts and ginger in the processor and process until coarsely chopped. Mix with half of the batter. Mix the chopped mixed peel with the remaining batter. Remove and wash the processor bowl.

Heat a frying or pancake pan with a little oil and when sizzling pour in 2 tablespoons of the batter. Cook until golden, flip over and cook until the underside is golden. Remove and keep warm on a plate set over a pan of simmering water.

Repeat the process using all the batter to produce 14 10cm/4in pancakes about 5mm/¼in thick.

Fit the plastic blade. Place the yoghurt, soured cream, lemon juice and sugar in the processor and process until smooth and blended. Serve with the warm pudding pancakes.

Pear sticky gingerbread pudding

Serves: 4–6
Attachment: plastic blade

Topping:
2 Conference pears
50g/2oz unsalted butter
2 tablespoons caster sugar

Gingerbread:
100g/4oz butter or margarine
175g/6oz black treacle
50g/2oz golden syrup
50g/2oz soft brown sugar
150ml/¼ pint milk
2 eggs, beaten
225g/8oz plain flour
1½ teaspoons mixed spice
1½ teaspoons ground ginger
1 teaspoon bicarbonate of soda
glacé cherries and angelica leaves to decorate

Grease a 20cm/8in round cake tin. Peel, core and slice the pears evenly. Arrange the slices in a circle on the base of the tin.

Fit the plastic blade. Place the butter and caster sugar in the processor bowl and process until blended, about 3 seconds. Spread carefully over the pears.

Put the butter or margarine, treacle, golden syrup and brown sugar in a pan. Heat gently until melted. Add the milk, blending well, cool slightly then stir in the beaten eggs.

Place the flour, spices and soda in the processor bowl and process for 2 seconds to blend. With the motor running, add the treacle mixture through the feed tube and process until well blended, about 6–8 seconds. Carefully pour over the pears.

Bake in a preheated cool oven (150°C, 300°F, gas mark 2) for 1¼–1½ hours or until a skewer inserted into the cake comes out clean. Allow to shrink in the tin slightly before inverting on a plate to serve. Decorate with glacé cherries and angelica leaves.

Upside-down orange pudding with orange foam sauce

Serves: 6
Attachments: metal blade, whipping blade (optional)

1 tablespoon golden syrup
sliced flesh of 3 oranges
rind of 2 oranges
75g/3oz butter or margarine
75g/3oz caster sugar
1 egg
150g/5oz self-raising flour
juice of 1 orange

Sauce:
rind of 1 orange
15g/½oz flour
50g/2oz caster sugar
25g/1oz butter
juice of 1 orange
1 egg, separated

Cover the base of a round, medium-sized, ovenproof dish with the syrup. Arrange the sliced oranges on the base and up the sides of the dish.

Fit the metal blade. Place the orange rind in the processor bowl and process until finely chopped. Add the butter, sugar, egg, flour, and orange juice. Process until well blended, about 8–10 seconds. Carefully spoon into the dish and bake in a preheated moderate oven (180°C, 350°F, gas mark 4) for 40 minutes. Rinse the processor bowl.

Fit the metal blade. Place the orange rind, flour, caster sugar, butter, orange juice and egg yolk in the processor bowl and process until smooth. Pour into a saucepan and cook until thickened. Rinse the processor bowl.

Fit the whipping blade and whip the egg white until it stands in stiff peaks. Alternatively, whisk the egg white until stiff. Fold into the orange sauce with a metal spoon.

To serve, invert the pudding on to a serving plate and serve at once with the orange foam sauce.

Lemon baked apples

Serves: 4
Attachment: metal blade

4 medium cooking apples
50g/2oz stoned dates
4 tablespoons Demerara sugar
4 tablespoons lemon curd
large knob of butter
4 tablespoons water

Wash and core the apples. Make a shallow cut around the middle of each to prevent them from bursting during cooking. Stand in a shallow ovenproof dish.

Fit the metal blade. Place the dates in the processor bowl and process until chopped, about 3 seconds. Add the sugar and lemon curd and process for 1–2 seconds to mix.

Stuff the apples with the date mixture and dot with the butter. Pour the water around the apples and bake in a preheated moderately hot oven (200°C, 400°F, gas mark 6) for 35-40 minutes until tender. Serve hot.

Orange and apricot tango

Serves: 6
Attachment: metal blade

1 × 425g/15oz can apricot halves, drained
rind of 5 oranges
flesh of 5 oranges
175g/6oz sugar
150ml/¼ pint water
juice of 1 small lemon

Fit the metal blade. Place the apricots, orange rind and orange flesh in the processor bowl and process until smooth, about 15 seconds.

Dissolve the sugar in the water then bring to the boil and cook for 5 minutes. Allow to cool then add to the processor bowl. Add the lemon juice and process to blend, about 5 seconds.

Pour into a freezer tray and freeze for 2 hours, without stirring. Scoop out and serve in glasses with crisp dessert biscuits if liked.

Mixed fruit crunch

Serves: 4
Attachments: slicing disc, metal blade

Filling:
450g/1lb cooking apples, peeled, cored and quartered
1 × 539g/1lb 13oz can rhubarb, drained
15g/½oz demerara sugar

Topping:
25g/1oz mixed nuts
175g/6oz plain flour
75g/3oz butter, cubed
25g/1oz demerara sugar

Fit the slicing disc. Slice the apples through the disc, and layer in an ovenproof dish with the rhubarb. Sprinkle with the sugar. Rinse and dry the processor bowl.

Fit the metal blade. Place the nuts in the processor bowl and process to chop, about 4 seconds. Remove and set aside.

Place the flour and butter in the processor bowl and process until the mixture resembles fine breadcrumbs, about 5–7 seconds. Add the sugar and nuts and process for a further 2 seconds to mix.

Spoon over the fruit filling and level the surface. Bake in a preheated moderate oven (180°C, 350°F, gas mark 4) for 45–60 minutes or until the fruit is cooked and the crumble topping is golden. Serve hot with custard or cream.

Greengage and plum cobbler

Serves: 4
Attachment: metal blade

225g/8oz self-raising flour
50g/2oz butter, diced
25g/1oz sugar
1 egg
5–6 tablespoons milk
450g/1lb ripe plums, halved and stoned
450g/1lb ripe greengages, halved and stoned
4 tablespoons clear honey
milk to glaze
sugar to sprinkle

Fit the metal blade. Place the flour and butter in the processor bowl and process for 5 seconds or until well mixed and blended. Add the sugar and process for a further 1 minute to mix.

With the motor running, add the egg and milk through the feed tube and process to form a soft dough. Roll out on a lightly-floured surface to about 2cm/¾in thick. Cut out scones with a 5cm/2in scone cutter and set aside.

Place the plums, greengages and honey in an ovenproof dish. Cover with foil and cook in a preheated moderately hot oven (200°C, 400°F, gas mark 6) for 15 minutes.

Remove the dish from the oven and allow to cool slightly. Arrange the scones in overlapping circles on top of the fruit. Brush with a little milk to glaze and sprinkle with a little sugar.

Return to the oven and cook for a further 30 minutes until well-risen and golden. Serve piping hot with fresh cream.

Vegetables and salads

Rösti with mushrooms

Serves: 4
Attachments: grating disc, metal blade

450g/1lb potatoes, peeled
4 sprigs parsley
½ onion, peeled
25g/1oz mushrooms
salt and freshly ground black pepper
pinch of ground nutmeg
1 tablespoon oil
15g/½oz butter

Cook the potatoes in boiling salted water for 5 minutes. Drain thoroughly.

Fit the grating disc. Cut the potatoes to fit the feed tube and grate through the disc. Remove and place in a bowl. Rinse the processor bowl.

Fit the metal blade. Place the parsley in the processor bowl and process for 4 seconds to chop. Add the onion and process for a further 3 seconds. Add the mushrooms and process for a further 2–3 seconds. Mix with the potatoes, adding salt, pepper and nutmeg to taste.

Heat the oil and butter in a large frying pan. Add the rösti mixture and flatten with a fork. Cook over a moderate heat for 8 minutes, turn over and cook for a further 8 minutes. Serve hot, cut into wedges.

Layered mushroom and tomato pancakes

Serves: 4
Attachments: metal blade, slicing disc

Pancake batter:
100g/4oz plain flour
pinch of salt
1 egg
1 tablespoon oil
300ml/½ pint milk
oil for cooking

Mushroom filling:
100g/4oz button mushrooms
25g/1oz butter
1 tablespoon flour
150ml/¼ pint single cream
salt and freshly ground black pepper

Tomato filling:
1 × 227g/8oz can plum tomatoes
2 tablespoons tomato pureé
1 small onion, peeled
small bunch of fresh basil leaves or 1 teaspoon dried basil
salt and freshly ground black pepper

Fit the metal blade. Prepare the pancake batter by placing the flour, salt, egg, oil and half of the milk in the processor and process for 15 seconds. Add the remaining milk and process for a further 15 seconds. Pour into a large jug. Remove and wash processor bowl.

Fit the slicing disc. Slice the mushrooms for the mushroom filling through the disc. Heat the butter in a pan, add the mushrooms, and cook for 3–5 minutes until softened. Stir in the flour blending well, and cook for 1 minute. Gradually add the cream and season with salt and pepper to taste. Cook for 3–5 minutes or until thickened. Set aside.

To make the tomato sauce, fit the metal blade. Place all the ingredients in the processor and process until well chopped but still chunky, about 5 seconds.

To make the pancakes, heat a 18cm/7in omelette or frying pan until hot then add just a smear of oil. Pour in a little of the batter and swirl to coat the bottom of the pan. Cook until the underside of the pancake is golden, flip over and cook the other side. Remove and stack on sheets of greaseproof paper. Repeat with the remaining mixture to make 8 pancakes.

Place one pancake in the base of a greased 18cm/7in cake tin. Top with a quarter of the tomato filling. Cover with a second pancake and top with a layer of mushroom filling. Continue layering in this way, finishing with a layer of mushroom filling.

Cook in a preheated moderately hot oven (190°C, 375°F, gas mark 5) for 15–20 minutes until golden and bubbly. Carefully remove from the tin and serve hot, cut into wedges, with salad.

Cucumber raita

Serves: 4
Attachments: grating disc, metal blade

½ cucumber, peeled
4 sprigs fresh mint
1 green chilli, seeded
150ml/¼ pint natural yoghurt
¼ teaspoon chilli powder
salt and freshly ground black pepper

Fit the grating disc. Cut the cucumber to feed the feed tube and grate the cucumber through the disc. Remove and set aside.

Fit the metal blade. Place the mint and chilli in the processor bowl and process until finely chopped. Add the yoghurt, chilli powder and seasoning to taste and process for 2 seconds to mix.

Fold in the grated cucumber and spoon into a serving dish. Serve with curries as a side dish.

Knockwurst and potato bake

Serves: 4
Attachment: slicing disc

225g/8oz knockwurst
350g/12oz onions, peeled and halved
675g/1½lb potatoes, peeled
salt and freshly ground black pepper
2 teaspoons dried rosemary
150ml/¼ pint chicken stock
1 tablespoon grated Parmesan cheese

Fit the slicing disc. Slice the knockwurst through the disc. Remove and set aside.

Slice the onions through the disc, remove and set aside. Cut the potatoes, if necessary, to fit the feed tube and slice through the disc. Remove and set aside.

Arrange thin layers of onion, potato and knockwurst in a medium-sized greased ovenproof dish, seasoning each layer with salt, pepper and a little rosemary, finishing with a layer of potato.

Pour the chicken stock over the mixture and cover with a lid or buttered foil. Cook in a preheated moderate oven (180°C, 350°F, gas mark 4) for 2½ hours.

About 30 minutes before the end of the cooking time, remove the lid or foil and sprinkle with Parmesan cheese. Continue to cook, uncovered, for the remaining time. Serve hot.

Herefordshire red cabbage

Serves: 4
Attachment: slicing disc

450g/1lb red cabbage, coarse outer leaves removed and cored
225g/8oz dessert apples, peeled, cored and quartered
5 tablespoons apple juice
pinch of caster sugar
½ teaspoon salt
4 cloves
3 tablespoons vinegar
25g/1oz butter
1½ teaspoons redcurrant jelly
salt and freshly ground black pepper

Fit the slicing disc. Cut the red cabbage to fit the feed tube and slice through the disc. Remove and place in a pan.

Slice the apples through the disc and place in the pan with the apple juice, sugar, salt and cloves. Cover and simmer for about 20 minutes.

Remove and discard the cloves. Add the vinegar, butter and redcurrant jelly, blending well. Reheat gently, season to taste with salt and pepper and serve hot.

Chinese style vegetables in spicy chilli sauce

Serves: 4
Attachments: slicing disc, metal blade

Vegetables:
50g/2oz canned water chestnuts
50g/2oz cucumber
50g/2oz mushrooms
1 red pepper, cored and seeded
1 carrot, peeled
100g/4oz beansprouts
50g/2oz canned bamboo shoots

Sauce:
½ onion, peeled
2 tablespoons sesame oil

¼ teaspoon Chinese 5-spice powder
pinch of ground ginger
150ml/¼ pint pineapple juice
1½ teaspoons hot chilli sauce
1 tablespoon soy sauce
1 tablespoon tomato purée
pinch of brown sugar
1 teaspoon cornflour

Fit the slicing disc. Slice the water chestnuts, cucumber, mushrooms, pepper and carrot through the disc. Remove and set aside.

Fit the metal blade. Place the onion in the processor bowl and process for about 3 seconds to chop.

Heat half of the oil in a pan. Add the onion and cook for 4 minutes. Add the spices and cook for 1 minute. Add all the remaining sauce ingredients except cornflour, blending well. Bring to the boil and cook for 1 minute. Mix the cornflour with a little water and stir into the sauce, blending well. Cook until clear and thickened.

Heat the remaining oil in a frying pan or wok and add the sliced vegetables. Stir-fry for 3 minutes. Add the beansprouts and bamboo shoots and stir-fry for a further 1 minute.

Add the sauce, toss lightly to blend, and serve at once.

Winter vegetables au gratin

Serves: 4
Attachments: slicing disc, metal blade

225g/8oz parsnips, peeled
225g/8oz carrots, peeled
225g/8oz swedes, peeled

Sauce:
½ onion, peeled
25g/1oz butter
25g/1oz flour
300ml/½ pint milk
salt and freshly ground white pepper

Fit the slicing disc. Cut the parsnips, carrots and swedes to fit the feed tube if necessary and slice through the disc. Cook in boiling salted water until tender, about 15 minutes. Drain thoroughly.

Meanwhile, fit the metal blade. Place the onion in the processor bowl and process for about 3 seconds to chop.

Melt the butter in a pan. Add the onion and cook for 5 minutes. Stir in the flour and cook for 1 minute. Gradually add the milk and bring to the boil, stirring constantly. Cook for 2–3 minutes. Add the cooked vegetables and salt and pepper to taste.

Spoon into a flameproof dish and cook under a preheated hot grill until golden and bubbly. Serve at once.

Pan haggarty

Serves: 4
Attachments: slicing disc, grating disc

450g/1lb potatoes, peeled
225g/8oz onions, peeled
100g/4oz Cheddar cheese
salt and freshly ground black pepper
ground nutmeg
dry mustard powder
3 tablespoons oil

Fit the slicing disc. Cut the potatoes and onion to fit the feed tube if necessary. Slice the potatoes and onion through the disc. Remove and set aside.

Fit the grating disc. Cut the cheese to fit the feed tube if necessary and grate through the disc. Mix the potatoes and onions with the cheese, salt, pepper, nutmeg and mustard to taste.

Heat the oil in a large frying pan. Add the potato mixture and level with a fork. Cook, over a moderate heat, for 7–10 minutes or until potato is almost cooked.

Remove from hob and cook under a preheated hot grill until golden and bubbly. Serve hot, cut into wedges from the pan.

Peperonata

Serves: 4
Attachment: slicing disc

1 large green pepper, cored and seeded
1 large red pepper, cored and seeded
1 large yellow pepper, cored and seeded
1 onion, peeled and quartered
1 clove garlic, peeled
3 tablespoons oil
1 teaspoon dried mixed herbs
4 tablespoons water
1 tablespoon Worcestershire sauce
1 tablespoon tomato purée
salt and freshly ground black pepper

Fit the slicing disc. Cut the peppers to fit the feed tube and slice through the disc. Slice the onion and garlic through the disc.

Heat the oil in a large pan. Add the pepper, onion and garlic mixture and herbs and cook for 5 minutes until softened.

Add the water, Worcestershire sauce, tomato purée and salt and pepper to taste. Cover with a tight-fitting lid and cook for 10–15 minutes until soft. Serve hot or cold.

Chunky green and grape salad

Serves: 4
Attachments: slicing disc, metal or plastic blade

225g/8oz cucumber
4 sticks celery, scrubbed
225g/8oz green grapes, halved and seeded
2 tablespoons natural yoghurt
2 tablespoons unsweetened apple juice
2 tablespoons chive mustard
salt and freshly ground black pepper

Fit the slicing disc. Cut the cucumber to fit the processor tube if necessary and slice through the slicing disc. Slice the celery through the slicing disc and transfer the cucumber and celery to a salad bowl.

Add the grapes and toss well to blend.

Fit the metal or plastic blade. Place the yoghurt, apple juice, mustard, and salt and pepper to taste in the processor and process for 3–5 seconds to blend.

Pour over the salad and toss well to coat. Serve at once as a delicious side salad.

Pastrami and beetroot salad

Serves: 4
Attachments: metal blade, slicing disc, plastic blade

100g/4oz walnut halves
450g/1lb cooked beetroot, peeled
175g/6oz pasta shapes, cooked according to packet instructions
3 tablespoons creamed horseradish
150ml/¼ pint soured cream
2 tablespoons orange juice
salt and fresly ground black pepper
225g/8oz thinly sliced pastrami
1 tablespoon scissor-snipped chives to garnish

Fit the metal blade. Place the walnuts in the processor bowl and process for 2–3 seconds to chop coarsely. Remove and place in a mixing bowl.

Fit the slicing disc. Cut the beetroot to fit the feed tube and slice through the disc. Remove and add to the walnuts with the pasta shapes. Rinse the processor bowl.

Fit the plastic blade. Place the horseradish, soured cream, orange juice and salt and pepper to taste in the processor bowl and process for 2–3 seconds to blend. Pour over the pasta salad and toss lightly to coat.

On a serving plate, arrange the slices of pastrami attractively. Pile the pasta salad into the centre of the dish and sprinkle with the chives. Serve at once.

Beef ploughboy

Serves: 4
Attachments: slicing disc, plastic blade

1 small red cabbage, coarse outer leaves removed and cored
1 onion, peeled and quartered
450g/1lb cooked roast beef
2 tablespoons dark treacle or molasses
4 tablespoons white wine vinegar
1 teaspoon made mustard
salt and freshly ground black pepper

Fit the slicing disc. Cut the red cabbage to fit the feed tube and slice through the disc. Slice the onion through the disc and remove both vegetables into a large salad bowl.

Slice the beef into thin strips and place in the salad bowl.

Fit the plastic blade. Place the treacle or molasses, vinegar, mustard, and salt and pepper to taste in the processor bowl and process for 4 seconds to blend.

Pour over the salad mixture and toss until the mixture is thoroughly combined. Serve at once with crusty bread.

Cucumber and herring salad

Serves: 4
Attachments: slicing disc, metal blade

½ medium cucumber
2 red dessert apples, cored and quartered
1 bunch spring onions, trimmed
3 tablespoons mayonnaise (see page 89)
1½ teaspoons creamed horseradish
2 tablespoons soured cream
1 × 340ml/12fl oz jar pickled herrings, drained

Fit the slicing disc. Slice the cucumber through the disc. Slice the apples through the disc and place both in a bowl.

Fit the metal blade. Place the spring onions in the processor bowl and process until finely chopped. Add to the salad bowl with the sultanas.

Place the mayonnaise, horseradish and soured cream in the processor bowl and process for 2 seconds to blend.

Cut the herrings into thin strips and add to the cucumber mixture. Add the dressing and toss well to mix. Spoon on to a chilled serving dish and serve at once with warm crusty bread.

Fruity coleslaw

Serves: 6–8
Attachments: slicing disc, grating disc, metal blade

1 small head white cabbage, cored and quartered
2 red-skinned eating apples, cored and quartered
2 celery stalks
3 carrots, peeled
50g/2oz walnut halves
75g/3oz fresh or canned pineapple (optional)
25g/1oz sultanas
150ml/¼ pint mayonnaise (see page 00)
50ml/2fl oz soured cream
salt and freshly ground pepper

Fit the slicing disc. Cut the cabbage to fit the feed tube and slice through the disc. Slice the apples and celery through the disc and place all three in a serving bowl.

Fit the grating disc. Grate the carrots through the disc and add to the apple mixture.

Fit the metal blade. Place the walnuts in the processor bowl and process for 2 seconds to chop coarsely. Add to the salad bowl. Add the pineapple to the processor bowl and process for 2 seconds to chop. Add to the salad bowl with the sultanas.

Place the mayonnaise and soured cream in the processor bowl with salt and pepper to taste. Process for 2 seconds to blend.

Pour over the coleslaw ingredients and toss well to coat. Serve as soon as possible.

Crunchy potato salad

Serves: 4
Attachments: slicing disc, metal blade

675g/1½lb cooked small waxy potatoes

1 large cucumber, halved lengthways
100g/4oz cooked ham
1 small onion, peeled
4 sprigs fresh dill
300ml/½ pint soured cream
2 teaspoons herb-flavoured mustard
salt and freshly ground black pepper
50g/2oz walnuts

Fit the slicing disc. Slice the potatoes through the disc. Remove and place in a salad bowl.

Slice the cucumber through the disc and add to the potatoes.

Fit the metal blade. Place the ham, onion and dill in the processor bowl and process until very coarsely chopped, about 1–2 seconds. Add to the potato mixture and toss well to blend.

Place the soured cream, mustard and salt and pepper to taste in the processor bowl and process for 2 seconds to blend.

Fold into or spoon over the salad. Crumble the walnuts with your fingers and sprinkle over the salad to serve.

Russian salad

Serves: 4
Attachments: slicing disc, metal blade

½ onion, peeled
1 stick celery
450g/1lb cooked waxy potatoes
75g/3oz cooked carrots
75g/3oz cooked beetroot (optional)
25g/1oz cooked sweetcorn kernels
75g/3oz cooked peas

Dressing:
150ml/¼ pint soured cream
3 tablespoons mayonnaise
2 teaspoons creamed horseradish
salt and freshly ground pepper

Fit the slicing disc. Slice the onion and celery through the disc and place in a bowl.

Fit the metal blade. Place the potatoes in the processor bowl and process until very coarsely chopped, about 2–4 seconds. Remove and add to the onion and celery mixture.

Add the carrots to the processor bowl and process until chopped, about 4 seconds. Remove and add to the salad bowl. Add the beetroot, if used, to the processor bowl and process to chop coarsely. Remove and add to the salad bowl. Rinse the processor bowl.

Fit the metal blade. Place all the dressing ingredients in the processor bowl and process for 3 seconds to blend. Pour over the salad ingredients. Add the sweetcorn and peas and toss well to mix.

Serve with cold roast meats, delicatessen sausages or cold table specialities.

Italian pasta salad

Serves: 4
Attachments: slicing disc, metal blade

1 onion, peeled and quartered
1 green pepper, cored and seeded
1 red pepper, cored and seeded
175g/6oz garlic sausage
225g/8oz pasta twists
about 12 black olives, stoned

Dressing:
2 tablespoons red wine vinegar
4 tablespoons oil
½ teaspoon dried oregano
pinch of mustard powder
pinch of caster sugar
salt and freshly ground black pepper

Fit the slicing disc. Slice the onion through the disc. Remove and set aside.

Fit the metal blade. Place the peppers in the processor bowl and process for about 4 seconds to chop. Remove and set aside.

Place the garlic sausage in the processor bowl and process to chop coarsely, about 2–4 seconds. Remove and set aside.

Cook the pasta in boiling salted water until cooked, about

12–15 minutes. Drain thoroughly. Allow to cool.

Place all the dressing ingredients in the processor bowl and process for 4 seconds to blend.

Add the onion, peppers, garlic sausage, pasta and olives and process for 4 seconds to mix. Serve lightly chilled.

Curried bean salad

Serves: 2–4
Attachment: metal blade

25g/1oz dried apricots
2 sticks celery
½ small red pepper, cored and seeded
½ small green pepper, cored and seeded
25g/1oz sultanas
275g/10oz cooked blackeye beans

Dressing:
2 tablespoons oil
1 tablespoon wine vinegar
pinch of dry mustard
pinch of sugar
½ teaspoon curry powder
1 tablespoon light soy sauce
salt and freshly ground black pepper

Fit the metal blade. Place the apricots in the processor bowl and process until chopped, about 4 seconds. Remove and place in a salad bowl.

Place the celery and peppers in the processor bowl and process until chopped, about 5 seconds. Add to the salad bowl with the sultanas and blackeye beans.

Place all the dressing ingredients in the processor bowl and process for 5 seconds to blend. Pour over the salad mixture and toss well to blend. Serve at once.

Sauces, marinades, dressings, stuffings, butters and glazes

Mushroom and lemon sauce

Serves: 4
Attachment: metal blade

pared rind of ½ lemon
225g/8oz button mushrooms
15g/½oz butter

15g/½oz flour
300ml/½ pint milk
salt and freshly ground pepper

Fit the metal blade. Place the lemon rind in the processor and
process until very finely chopped.

Add the mushrooms and process until coarsely chopped,
about 5 seconds.

Melt the butter in a pan. Add the lemon and mushroom
mixture and cook until softened, about 5 minutes.

Stir in the flour, blending well, and cook for 1 minute.
Gradually add the milk, bring to the boil and cook, stirring for 2
minutes.

Season to taste with salt and pepper and serve hot with grilled
or barbecued meat and fish.

Chilli barbecue sauce

Serves: 4
Attachment: metal blade

1 small onion, peeled
15g/½oz butter
150ml/¼ pint tomato ketchup
3 tablespoons Worcestershire sauce
1 teaspoon chilli powder
150ml/¼ pint wine vinegar
2 tablespoons clear honey
3 tablespoons water
1 teaspoon made mustard
salt and freshly ground black pepper

Fit the metal blade. Place the onion in the processor and process
until finely chopped.

Melt the butter in a pan, add the onions and fry until
softened, about 5 minutes.

Add the tomato ketchup, Worcestershire sauce, chilli powder,
wine vinegar, honey, water and mustard, blending well. Season
to taste with salt and pepper and bring to the boil. Lower the
heat and simmer for 5 minutes.

Serve hot with grilled or barbecued meat, poultry or sausages.

Easy red wine and mushroom sauce

Makes: about 300ml/½ pint
Attachment: metal blade

75g/3oz mushrooms
25g/1oz butter
6 tablespoons red wine
150ml/¼ pint beef stock
dash of Worcestershire sauce
salt and freshly ground black pepper
2–3 teaspoons cornflour

Fit the metal blade. Place the mushrooms in the processor bowl and process until finely chopped, about 5 seconds.

Heat the butter in a pan. Add the mushrooms and cook until softened, about 5 minutes.

Add the red wine, stock, Worcestershire sauce and salt and pepper to taste. Cook for 2 minutes.

Mix the cornflour with a little water and stir into the sauce. Heat, stirring constantly, until clear and thickened. Use as required.

Serve with grills and roasts.

Cheese and spinach sauce

Serves: 4
Attachment: metal blade

100g/4oz spinach leaves, sorted and washed
25g/1oz butter
25g/1oz flour
300ml/½ pint milk
40g/1½oz Cheddar cheese, grated
salt and freshly ground black pepper
ground nutmeg

Place the spinach in a pan with just the water from washing clinging to the leaves. Cover and cook until tender, about 4 minutes.

Fit the metal blade. Place the spinach in the processor bowl and process until finely chopped, about 6 seconds.

Melt the butter in a pan. Add the flour and cook for 1 minute. Gradually add the milk and bring to the boil, stirring constantly. Cook for 2 minutes.

Stir in the spinach, cheese, salt, pepper and nutmeg to taste, blending well. Cook over a low heat until the cheese melts.

Serve with cooked beans or as a sauce to top gratin-baked pasta.

Mayonnaise

Makes: about 300ml/½ pint
Attachment: metal blade

3 egg yolks
½ teaspoon salt
½ teaspoon mustard powder
pinch of cayenne pepper
7 teaspoons white wine vinegar or lemon juice
300ml/½ pint olive, safflower or sunflower oil

Fit the metal blade. Place the egg yolks, salt, mustard powder, cayenne pepper and 3 teaspoons of the vinegar or lemon juice in the processor bowl and process until well mixed, about 3 seconds.

With the motor running, add the oil, through the feed tube, in a slow, steady stream – the mayonnaise produced will be thick and glossy.

Add the remaining vinegar or lemon juice and use as required.

Orange mayonnaise

Makes: 300ml/½ pint
Attachment: metal blade

rind of ½ orange
250ml/8fl oz mayonnaise (see above)
2 teaspoons caster sugar
4 teaspoons Grand Marnier
2 tablespoons orange juice

Fit the metal blade. Place the orange rind in the processor bowl and process until very finely chopped, about 6–8 seconds.

Add the mayonnaise, sugar, Grand Marnier and orange juice and process for 3–4 seconds to blend.

Chill thoroughly before serving with rice salads, coleslaw or fruit salads.

Apple and horseradish mayonnaise

Makes: about 300ml/½ pint
Attachments: grating disc, plastic blade

1 small dessert apple, peeled, cored and quartered
2 teaspoons lemon juice
200ml/7fl oz mayonnaise (see page 89)
2½ teaspoons dry white wine
2 teaspoons creamed horseradish
salt and freshly ground pepper

Fit the grating disc. Grate the apple through the disc.

Fit the plastic blade. Add the lemon juice and process for 1 second to blend.

Add the mayonnaise, wine, horseradish and salt and pepper to taste and process for 3 seconds to blend.

Serve with smoked fish or beef.

Spicy orange marinade

Makes: about 300ml/½ pint
Attachments: metal blade, juice extractor (optional)

1 large orange
150ml/¼ pint dry white wine
2 tablespoons soy sauce
¼ teaspoon ground ginger
2 tablespoons oil
1 tablespoon brown sugar

Fit the metal blade. Thinly peel the rind from the orange, place in the processor and process until finely chopped, about 1 minute.

Remove the pith from the orange and any pips. Squeeze the juice into the processor or use the juice extractor if your machine has this attachment.

Add the wine, soy sauce, ginger, oil and sugar. Process using the metal blade for 3–5 seconds to mix.

Use as a delicious marinade or baste for lamb or pork.

Cider marinade

Makes: about 300ml/½ pint
Attachment: metal blade

1 onion, peeled and quartered
1 clove garlic, peeled
2 teaspoons dried mixed herbs
4 tablespoons cider
1 tablespoon lemon juice
salt and freshly ground black pepper

Fit the metal blade. Place the onion, garlic, herbs, cider, lemon juice and salt and pepper to taste in the processor bowl and process until the onion is finely chopped, about 4 seconds.

Use to marinate chicken, turkey or pork dishes.

Red devil marinade

Makes: about 100ml/4fl oz
Attachment: metal blade

1 small onion, peeled and quartered
2 tablespoons apricot jam
4 tablespoons tomato ketchup
1 tablespoon soy sauce
2 teaspoons made French mustard
1 tablespoon Worcestershire sauce
1 tablespoon lemon juice
1 tablespoon ground paprika

Fit the metal blade. Place all the ingredients in the processor bowl and process until smooth, about 10 seconds.

Use as a marinade and basting sauce for burgers, chicken portions and sausages.

Cranberry marinade

Makes: about 300ml/½ pint
Attachment: metal blade

½ small onion, peeled
8 tablespoons cranberry jelly
2 tablespoons lemon juice
2 teaspoons ground mace
4 tablespoons oil

Fit the metal blade. Place all the ingredients in the processor bowl and process until smooth, about 8 seconds.

Use as a marinade and basting sauce for turkey, duck, chicken and sausages.

Brown ale marinade

Makes: 450ml/¾ pint
Attachment: metal blade

1 large onion, peeled
small bunch mixed fresh herbs
2 teaspoons made English mustard
1 × 300ml/½ pint can brown ale
75ml/3fl oz oil

Fit the metal blade. Place the onion and herbs in the processor bowl and process until finely chopped.

Add the mustard, brown ale and oil and process for 2–3 seconds to mix.

Use as a marinade for beef roasts and steaks.

Apricot stuffing balls

Makes: 12 balls
Attachment: metal blade

175g/6oz dried apricots
100g/4oz celery stalks
175g/6oz white bread

92

½ teaspoon dried sage
¼ teaspoon mixed spice
salt and freshly ground black pepper
1 teaspoon Dijon mustard
25g/1oz melted butter
1 egg, beaten
oil for cooking

Fit the metal blade. Place the apricots and celery in the processor bowl and process until finely chopped, about 5 seconds. Remove and set aside.

Place the bread in the processor bowl and process until breadcrumbs are made. Add the apricot and celery mixture, sage, mixed spice, salt and pepper to taste, mustard, butter and egg and process until well blended, about 3–5 seconds. Divide and shape into 12 stuffing balls.

Lightly oil a small roasting tin and add the stuffing balls. Cook in a preheated moderate oven (160°C, 325°F, gas mark 3) for 30–35 minutes. Delicious served as an accompaniment to pork.

Fruit and nut stuffing

Makes: enough to stuff 1 × 4.5kg/10lb goose or turkey
Attachment: metal blade

100g/4oz fresh white bread, cubed
2 large onions, peeled
4 large cooking apples, peeled, cored and quartered
175g/6oz dried apricots, soaked overnight
225g/8oz mixed shelled nuts (Brazils, walnuts and hazelnuts for example)
50g/2oz butter
350g/12oz pork sausagemeat
½ teaspoon dried marjoram
salt and freshly ground black pepper

Fit the metal blade. Add the bread cubes through the feed tube, with the motor running, to make breadcrumbs. Remove and set aside. Add the onion to the processor bowl and process until finely chopped. Remove and set aside.

Add the apples to the processor bowl and process until

coarsely chopped. Remove and set aside. Add the apricots to the processor bowl and process until finely chopped. Remove and set aside. Add the nuts to the processor bowl and process until coarsely chopped.

Melt the butter in a pan. Add the onion and cook for 5 minutes. Add the sausagemeat and cook for 5 minutes, stirring frequently to break up the meat. Cook for a further 5 minutes then stir in the breadcrumbs, apple, apricots, nuts, marjoram, and salt and pepper to taste, blending well. Cook for 3 minutes, stirring frequently.

Allow to cool then use to stuff the goose or turkey.

Prune, apple and almond stuffing

Makes: enough to stuff 1 large turkey or goose
Attachment: metal blade

1 onion, peeled and halved
3 medium cooking apples, peeled, cored and quartered
225g/8oz prunes, soaked overnight and stoned
rind of 1 small lemon
175g/6oz white bread, cubed
75g/3oz butter
turkey or goose liver
25g/1oz flaked almonds
juice of 1 small lemon
1 teaspoon ground cardamom
1 teaspoon dried marjoram
salt and freshly ground black pepper
4 tablespoons brandy

Fit the metal blade. Place the onion, apples and prunes in the processor bowl and process until chopped, about 5 seconds. Remove and set aside.

Place the lemon rind in the processor bowl and process until finely chopped. With the motor still running, add the bread cubes through the feed tube and process to make breadcrumbs. Remove and set aside.

Melt the butter in a pan and quickly fry the liver until cooked. Place with the cooking juices in the processor bowl and process until finely chopped. Add the onion, apple and prune mixture, breadcrumb and lemon mixture, almonds, lemon juice, cardamom, marjoram, salt and pepper to taste and brandy. Process until well blended, about 5–8 seconds.

Use to stuff a turkey or goose as required.

Cranberry stuffing

Makes: enough to stuff a small turkey or a large boned leg of lamb
Attachment: metal blade

rind of 1 lemon
4 sprigs parsley
175g/6oz fresh white bread, cubed
2 small onions, peeled
100g/4oz button mushrooms
4 tablespoons cranberry sauce
25g/1oz butter, melted
1 egg, beaten
salt and freshly ground black pepper

Fit the metal blade. Place the lemon rind and parsley in the processor bowl and process until finely chopped. With the motor running, add the bread through the feed tube, and make breadcrumbs. Remove and set aside.

Place the onions and mushrooms in the processor bowl and process until finely chopped, about 2–3 seconds. Add the breadcrumb mixture, cranberry sauce, butter, egg and salt and pepper to taste. Process until well mixed, about 5 seconds. Use as required.

Rice and watercress stuffing

Makes: enough to stuff 1 medium chicken
Attachment: metal blade

rind of 1 lemon
1 bunch watercress
50g/2oz walnut halves
100g/4oz streaky bacon, rinded
100g/4oz cooked long-grain rice
15g/½oz butter
1 large egg
salt and freshly ground black pepper

Fit the metal blade. Place the lemon rind in the processor bowl and process until finely chopped. Add the watercress and process until finely chopped, about 3 seconds. Add the walnuts and process for a further 2 seconds until coarsely chopped. Remove and set aside.

   Place the bacon in the processor bowl and process until finely chopped, about 3 seconds. Add the rice, watercress mixture, butter, egg and salt and pepper to taste. Process for 2–3 seconds to bind the stuffing mixture together. Use as required.

Chestnut stuffing

Makes: enough for 1 large chicken or medium turkey
Attachment: metal blade

3 sprigs parsley
50g/2oz fresh white bread, cubed
50g/2oz butter
1 turkey or chicken heart and liver
225g/8oz cooked chestnuts
2 sticks celery
100g/4oz bacon, rinded
salt and freshly ground black pepper

Fit the metal blade. Place the parsley in the processor bowl and process until finely chopped. With the motor running, add the bread through the feed tube to make breadcrumbs. Remove and set aside.

Meanwhile, melt the butter in a pan and lightly cook the liver and heart, about 5 minutes.

Place the chestnuts in the processor bowl and purée until smooth, about 15 seconds. Remove and set aside.

Place the celery, bacon, and liver and heart with their juices in the processor bowl and process until chopped, about 4 seconds.

Add the breadcrumbs, chestnut purée and salt and pepper to taste. Process until well blended, about 6 seconds. Use as required.

Plum stuffing

Makes: enough to stuff a large chicken or medium turkey
Attachment: metal blade

175g/6oz red plums, halved and stoned
450g/1lb pie veal, cubed
1 onion, peeled and quartered
225g/8oz pork sausagemeat
pinch of dried mixed herbs
salt and freshly ground black pepper

Fit the metal blade. Place the plums in the processor bowl and process to chop, about 3 seconds. Remove and set aside.

Place the veal in the processor bowl and process until minced, about 8 seconds. Add the onion and process for a further 2 seconds.

Add the sausagement, herbs, plums and salt and pepper to taste. Process for 2–3 seconds to blend. Use as required.

Blue cheese butter

Serves: 4
Attachment: metal or plastic blade

100g/4oz butter, diced
100g/4oz Stilton cheese
freshly ground black pepper

Fit the metal blade or plastic blade. Place the butter, cheese, and

pepper to taste in the processor bowl and process for 10 seconds.
Scrape down the bowl and process for a further 10 seconds.
Remove and store in the refrigerator until required.

Serve with gammon and beef steaks.

Lemon and parsley butter

Serves: 4
Attachment: metal blade

rind of ½ lemon
2 sprigs parsley
100g/4oz butter, diced
salt and freshly ground pepper

Fit the metal blade. Place the lemon rind and parsley in the
processor bowl and process until finely chopped, about 5–8
seconds.

Add the butter and salt and pepper to taste. Process for 10
seconds. Scrape down the bowl and process for a further 10
seconds. Store in the refrigerator until required.

Serve with fish and shellfish, grilled lamb or pork.

Garlic butter

Serves: 4 or makes enough for 1 French stick
Attachment: metal blade

2 cloves garlic, peeled
2 sprigs parsley
100g/4oz butter, diced
salt and freshly ground black pepper

Fit the metal blade. Place the garlic and parsley in the processor
bowl and process until finely chopped, about 5–8 seconds.

Add the butter and salt and pepper to taste. Process for 10
seconds. Scrape down the bowl and process for a further 10
seconds. Store, covered, in the refrigerator until required.

Serve with steaks and lamb chops or use to make garlic bread.

Honey and mustard glaze

Makes: enough to coat a 4kg/8–10lb leg of pork
Attachment: metal blade

1 clove garlic, peeled
3 tablespoons Dijon mustard
3 tablespoons clear honey
2 tablespoons oil
pinch of dried marjoram
pinch of dried sage
¼ teaspoon ground ginger
salt and freshly ground black pepper

Fit the metal blade. Place the garlic in the processor bowl and process until finely chopped.

Add the remaining ingredients and process until well blended, about 5 seconds.

Spread over the leg of pork and leave to stand for 2–3 hours. Roast, in a preheated moderate oven, (160°C, 325°F, gas mark 3) for 30 minutes per 450g/1lb plus 30 minutes.

Port and redcurrant glaze

Makes: enough to glaze 1 large turkey or duck
Attachment: metal blade

rind of ½ lemon
100ml/4fl oz port
4 tablespoons redcurrant jelly
¼ teaspoon ground nutmeg

Fit the metal blade. Place the lemon rind in the processor bowl and process until finely chopped.

Add the remaining ingredients and process for 5 seconds to blend.

Pour into a saucepan and bring to the boil. Boil for 10 minutes until syrupy. Use as required.

Juniper baste

Makes: enough to baste 1 large turkey
Attachment: metal blade

1 small onion, peeled
4 juniper berries
4 tablespoons oil
4 tablespoons white wine
½ teaspoon dried thyme

Fit the metal blade. Place the onion and juniper berries in the processor bowl and process until the onion is finely chopped and the juniper berries are lightly crushed or chopped.

Add the oil, wine and thyme and process for 2 seconds to blend. Use as required.

Dazzling decorations and garnishes

Cucumber slices and twists

Fit the slicing disc. Halve the cucumber lengthways, if necessary, to fit the feed tube and slice through the disc to give fine slices. Immature varieties need not be cut and can be sliced whole. Using a sharp knife, cut each slice from the edge to the centre, open and twist each slice in opposite directions to make cucumber twists. Decorate the centre with a sprig of herbs if liked.

Cucumber half-moons or wheels

Fit the slicing disc. Using a paring knife, thinly pare the cucumber along its length at regular intervals. Halve the cucumber lengthways to make half-moons, and use an immature cucumber for wheels. Slice the cucumber through the disc to make notched half-moons or notched 'wheels'.

Cucumber butterflies

Fit the slicing disc. Using a paring knife, thinly pare the cucumber along its length at regular intervals. Halve the cucumber lengthways and slice through the disc. Cut each half-moon slice from the outside peel edge almost into the centre and open to form a butterfly shape.

Pepper lattice

Fit the slicing disc. Core, de-seed and slice red, green or yellow peppers through the disc. Arrange over food to make a colourful lattice.

Sliced olives

Fit the slicing disc. Pimento-stuffed olives look very attractive if sliced through the disc to show their colourful red centres.

Vegetable nest

Fit the slicing disc. Shred crisp lettuce, cabbage, chinese leaves, mangetout, or small young beans through the disc to make an attractive edge to a salad dish.

Pepper bundles

Core and de-seed the pepper then remove one small slice horizontally from one end to make a pepper ring. Fit the slicing disc, cut the pepper to fit the feed tube and slice the pepper through the disc and gather together in a bundle. Push through the pepper ring to hold and secure.

Vegetable shapes

Peel carrots, turnips, swede or celeriac and cut into pieces that will fit the feed tube. Fit the slicing disc and slice through the disc. Cut out shapes from the sliced vegetables using canapé cutters or a sharp knife. Interesting shapes include hearts, moons, clovers, stars and flowers.

Chopped herbs

Fit the metal blade. With the motor running, drop sprigs of fresh herbs through the feed tube on to the metal blade and process until finely chopped. Use to sprinkle on soups and savoury dishes or use to make savoury butters.

Chopped nuts

Fit the metal blade. Place the chosen nuts in the processor bowl and process until coarsely or finely chopped, as liked.

Chopped peppers

Fit the metal blade. Place the cored and seeded peppers in the processor bowl and process until chopped. Sprinkle on soups or savoury dishes as a colourful garnish.

Whipped cream

This can only be done if your processor has a whipping blade – some processors are too powerful to whip sufficient air into the cream to stiffen for use. Fit the whipping blade and place the cream in the processor bowl, process until thick, according to manufacturer's instructions.

Orange, lemon, lime and grapefruit slices

Halve lemons, limes and oranges and quarter grapefruits to fit the feed tube. Fit the slicing disc and slice the fruit through the disc. Use as a garnish for drinks, desserts and fruit-flavoured dishes.

Game or potato chips

Peel potatoes and cut to fit the feed tube. Fit the slicing disc. Slice the potatoes through the disc, pat dry on absorbent kitchen towel then deep fry in hot oil until golden and crisp. Drain and sprinkle with salt. Use to garnish poultry and game dishes.

Butter icing

Fit the metal blade. Place 175g/6oz sifted icing sugar and 75g/3oz diced butter with any flavourings desired in the processor bowl and process until light and fluffy, about 15–20 seconds. Use to decorate cakes, biscuits and pastries.

Chopped glacé fruits and peel

Fit the metal blade. Place assorted glacé fruits and candied peel in the processor bowl and process until chopped. Use to decorate cakes, desserts, pastries, breads and biscuits as liked.

Chopped hard-boiled egg

Fit the metal blade. Place hard-boiled egg whites, yolks or both in the processor bowl and process until finely chopped. Use to sprinkle on savoury dishes.

Sliced strawberries, peaches, melon, etc.

Fit the slicing disc. Prepare fruit, i.e. hull, peel and stone or seed, and cut to fit the feed tube. Slice through the disc to make decorations for desserts, puddings and drinks – especially punches.

Chocolate chips

Fit the metal blade. Place the chocolate in the processor bowl and process for 10–12 seconds until finely chopped. Use to sprinkle on puddings and desserts, coat the sides of cakes, or use in ice creams.

Chocolate curls

Fit the grating disc. Use cooking chocolate with a fairly soft texture. Grate the chocolate through the disc to make small curls. Use to decorate cakes and gateaux.

Entertaining main meals and desserts

Citrus spatchcock poussins

Serves: 4
Attachment: metal blade

4 poussins, weighing about 275g/10oz each
2 lemons
2 tablespoons clear honey
salt and freshly ground black pepper
1 tablespoon safflower oil
lemon twists and watercress sprigs to garnish

Halve the poussins with scissors almost through and open out flat. Place in a shallow dish and make small deep cuts in the skin with a sharp knife.

Fit the metal blade. Thinly peel the rind from 1 lemon, place in the processor and process until finely chopped, about 1 minute.

Remove the rind and pith from the second lemon and pith from the first. Remove and discard any pips and place the flesh of both into the processor. Process until coarsely chopped.

Add the honey, salt and pepper to taste and oil. Process for 5 seconds to mix well.

Spread over the poussins, cover and chill for 4–6 hours.

To cook, remove the poussins from the marinade with a slotted spoon and place on a grill rack. Grill, under medium heat, for 15–25 minutes, turning and basting frequently with the marinade. Serve with a crisp seasonal salad.

Pork in peanut sauce

Serves: 4
Attachments: slicing disc, metal blade

1 small green pepper, cored, seeded and halved
1 large onion, peeled and quartered
2 cloves garlic, peeled
50g/2oz salted peanuts
2 tablespoons oil
450g/1lb pork fillet, cut into bite-sized cubes
½ teaspoon ground cumin
½ teaspoon ground coriander
1 teaspoon chilli powder
1 teaspoon ground ginger
5 tablespoons peanut butter
juice of ½ lemon
150ml/¼ pint water
freshly ground black pepper
chopped parsley to garnish

Fit the slicing disc. Slice the green pepper through the disc, remove and set aside.

Fit the metal blade. Place the onion and garlic in the processor bowl and process until coarsely chopped, about 3 seconds. Add the peanuts and process until coarsely chopped, about 3–4 seconds.

Heat the oil in a large pan. Add the pork and cook, over a high heat, until browned on all sides. Add the cumin, coriander, chilli powder and ginger, blending well. Cook for 1 minute.

Add the green pepper and onion and peanut mixture and cook for 2–3 minutes.

Add the peanut butter, lemon juice, water and pepper to taste, blending well. Cover and cook, over a gentle heat, for 15–20 minutes until the pork is cooked.

Adjust seasoning and serve with boiled rice. Garnish with chopped parsley.

Honeyed duck

Serves: 4
Attachment: metal blade

4 duck breast portions
1 clove garlic, peeled
1 × 2.5cm/1in piece fresh root ginger, peeled
4 tablespoons clear honey
2 tablespoons oil
2 tablespoons apple, pineapple or orange juice
salt and freshly ground black pepper

Remove the skin from the duck and make 3–4 deep cuts or slashes in each portion.

Fit the metal blade. Place the garlic and root ginger in the processor bowl and process until finely chopped, about 5 seconds.

Add the honey, oil, fruit juice and salt and pepper to taste. Marinade the duck in this mixture in the refrigerator for up to 24 hours, turning occasionally.

Remove the duck from the marinade with a slotted spoon. Cook under a preheated hot grill for 30 minutes, basting with the marinade, and turning regularly. Serve hot.

Chinese style sweet and sour prawns

Serves: 4
Attachment: metal blade

1 red pepper, cored and seeded
1 small bunch spring onions, trimmed
1 × 2.5cm/1in piece fresh root ginger, peeled
2 tablespoons oil
450g/1lb peeled prawns

Sauce:
2 tablespoons clear honey
1 tablespoon dry sherry
1 tablespoon soy sauce
1 tablespoon vinegar
2 teaspoons cornflour
2 tablespoons water
parsley or coriander sprigs to garnish

Fit the metal blade. Place the pepper, spring onions and ginger in the processor and process until coarsely chopped, about 3–5 seconds.

Heat the oil in a pan and add the chopped pepper mixture. Sauté for 2–3 minutes, or until the colours brighten, and stir in the prawns. Cook for 2–3 minutes or until heated through.

Place the sauce ingredients in the processor and process to blend thoroughly. Stir into the prawns and cook, stirring constantly, until the mixture thickens.

Serve at once on a bed of boiled rice and garnished with parsley or coriander sprigs.

Seafood au gratin

Serves: 6
Attachments: metal blade, grating disc

500g/1¼lb cooked potatoes
1½ tablespoons milk
50g/2oz butter
1 small onion, peeled
2 teaspoons cornflour

2 teaspoons mustard powder
2 tablespoons dry vermouth or white wine
150ml/¼ pint single cream
450g/1lb white fish fillet, skinned and cubed
100g/4oz seedless grapes
100g/4oz peeled prawns
salt and freshly ground pepper
40g/1½oz Cheddar or Gruyère cheese
2 tablespoons flaked almonds

Fit the metal blade. Place the potatoes, milk and half of the
butter in the processor and process until smooth and puréed,
about 4 to 6 seconds (time carefully, making sure not to over-
process). Remove and wash processor bowl.

Fit the metal blade. Place the onion in the processor and
process until finely chopped. Remove and wash the processor
bowl.

Melt the remaining butter in a pan. Add the onion and sauté
until transparent. Mix the cornflour, mustard powder and
vermouth or wine together and stir into the cream. Add to the
onion and bring slowly to a simmer, stirring constantly. Add the
fish cubes and simmer gently for 3 minutes.

Add the grapes, prawns and salt and pepper to taste, then
spoon into six individual dishes or scallop shells.

Spoon the potato mixture into a piping bag fitted with a large
star-shaped nozzle and pipe a potato border around the edge of
each dish.

Cook under a preheated hot grill until light golden.

Meanwhile, fit the grating disc and grate the cheese.

Sprinkle the seafood au gratin with the cheese and almonds
and cook for a further 2–3 minutes until golden and bubbly.
Serve at once.

Lamb masala

Serves: 4
Attachment: metal blade

Paste:
1 onion, peeled
3 cloves garlic, peeled
1 tablespoon coriander seeds
1 teaspoon ground ginger
1 teaspoon chilli powder
1½ teaspoons garam masala
1½ teaspoons turmeric
150ml/¼ pint natural yoghurt

Meat:
1 onion, peeled
2 tablespoons oil
6 lamb neck fillets, cubed
4 bay leaves
2 cardamoms
6 cloves
6 black peppercorns
1 teaspoon cumin seeds or ½ teaspoon cumin powder
1 cinnamon stick
4 tablespoons tomato purée
450ml/¾ pint well-flavoured stock

Fit the metal blade. Place all the paste ingredients in the processor bowl and process until finely chopped and almost smooth, about 15–20 seconds. Remove and set aside.

Place the onion in the processor bowl and process to chop, about 2 seconds.

Heat the oil in a large pan. Add the lamb and onion and cook over a high heat until browned on all sides. Add the herbs and spices and cook for 3 minutes. Gradually add the tomato purée and stock. Cover and cook, over a gentle heat, for 45 minutes.

Stir in the yoghurt paste, blending well and cook, over a low heat for a further 15 minutes.

Serve hot with Indian pilau rice, cucumber raita (see page 74) and/or a tomato and onion salad.

Honey and strawberry charlotte russe

Serves: 6
Attachment: metal blade

150ml/¼ pint made-up lemon jelly
6 candied lemon slices
angelica
24 sponge fingers
450g/1lb strawberries, hulled
2 tablespoons lemon juice
3 tablespoons clear honey
15g/½oz powdered gelatine
2 tablespoons hot water
450ml/¾ pint double cream

Lightly oil the bottom of a 1 litre/1¾ pint charlotte mould or other suitable mould or basin. Pour in a very thin layer of the lemon jelly and chill to set. Place the lemon slices and angelica in a decorative pattern on top of the jelly and pour over a little more jelly, being careful not to disturb the lemon and angelica from their positions. Chill to set.

Dip the sponge fingers in the remaining jelly and arrange upright around the sides of the mould, sugared sides outwards. Trim to fit and chill while preparing the filling.

Fit the metal blade. Place the strawberries, lemon juice and honey in the processor and blend until smooth.

Place the gelatine in a small bowl with the hot water and place the bowl in a saucepan of hot water. Heat until the gelatine is clear and dissolved. Add to the strawberries and process for 3–5 seconds to blend.

Whip the cream until it stands in soft peaks and fold into the strawberry mixture. Pour into the prepared charlotte mould and chill until set.

To serve, turn out of the mould on to a serving dish, dipping the mould briefly in hot water to loosen if necessary. Cut into wedges to serve.

Truffle dessert cake

Serves: 4–6
Attachments: metal blade, plastic blade

175g/6oz digestive or other plain biscuits, broken in half
500g/2oz toasted almonds
1 egg
25g/1oz sultanas
50g/2oz glacé cherries, halved
100g/4oz butter
100g/4oz soft brown sugar
3 tablespoons cocoa powder
2–3 tablespoons rum or brandy
150ml/¼ pint whipping cream

Fit the metal blade. Place the biscuits and almonds in the processor bowl and process until coarsely chopped, about 8 seconds

Fit the plastic blade and add the egg, sultanas and glacé cherries.

Melt the butter in a small pan. Stir in the sugar, cocoa and rum or brandy.

With the motor running, pour the butter down the feed tube and process to mix, about 20 seconds.

Spoon into a greased and lined 18cm/7in cake tin. Smooth the surface and chill to set.

Remove the cake from the tin and place on a serving dish. Whip the cream until it stands in soft peaks. Swirl or pipe on the cake decoratively. Cut into wedges to serve.

Brown bread ice cream

Serves: 6
Attachments: metal blade, whipping blade (optional)

75g/3oz wholemeal bread
50g/2oz hazelnuts
50g/2oz golden granulated sugar
3 egg whites
75g/3oz light muscovado sugar
300ml/½ pint double cream

Fit the metal blade. Place the bread and hazelnuts in the processor bowl and process until very finely chopped, about 10 seconds. Add the golden granulated sugar and process for 2 seconds to blend. Spread on a grill tray and cook under a preheated hot grill until crisp. Allow to cool. Rinse the processor bowl.

Meanwhile, fit the whipping blade, if available, and whip the egg whites until stiff. Alternatively, whisk the egg whites until they stand in stiff peaks. Add the sugar and process for 1 minute to mix. Remove and place in a bowl. Fold in the breadcrumb mixture with a metal spoon. Rinse the processor bowl.

Fit the whipping blade, if available, and whip the cream until just stiff. Alternatively, whisk the cream until it stands in soft peaks. Fold into the breadcrumb mixture with a metal spoon then transfer to a freezing tray. Freeze until firm, about 2 hours. Serve scooped into tall sundae glasses.

Roquefort and cherry cheesecake

Serves: 8
Attachment: metal blade

Base:
6 tablespoons cornflakes

Filling:
rind of ½ lemon
450g/1lb cream cheese
100g/4oz Roquefort cheese, cubed
175g/6oz caster sugar
3 eggs
2 tablespoons cornflour
2 tablespoons soured cream
pinch of salt
100g/4oz melted butter
1 × 430g/15oz can black cherries in syrup
1 tablespoon cherry brandy
2 teaspoons arrowroot powder

Fit the metal blade. Place the cornflakes in the processor bowl and process for 2–4 seconds until just crushed.

Generously butter a 20cm/8in loose-bottomed cake tin. Sprinkle the buttered base with the cornflakes. Rinse the processor bowl.

Fit the metal blade. Place the lemon rind in the processor and process until finely chopped. Add the cream cheese, Roquefort, sugar, eggs, cornflour, soured cream and salt. With the motor running, add the melted butter through the feed tube and process until well blended, about 10–12 seconds. Spoon over the cornflakes.

Bake in a preheated cool oven (150°C, 300°F, gas mark 2) for about 1½ hours. Turn the oven off and leave the cake to cook in the residual heat. When completely cold remove from the tin and place on a serving dish.

Stone and halve the cherries and arrange on top of the cheesecake. Place the cherry juice in a pan with the cherry brandy. Blend the arrowroot with a little cold water to make a paste and stir into the cherry juice. Bring to the boil, stirring constantly, until clear and thickened. Cool slightly then pour over the cherries to give a shiny glaze. Chill before serving.

Kiwi fruit ice cream

Serves: 8
Attachment: metal blade

150ml/¼ pint water
100g/4oz light muscovado sugar
juice of 1 lemon
6 ripe kiwi fruit, peeled
4 eggs
300ml/½ pint single cream
150ml/¼ pint double cream

Heat the water and sugar until boiling. Stir in the lemon juice then allow to cool.

Fit the metal blade. Place the kiwi fruit, sugar syrup, eggs and creams in the processor bowl and process until smooth. Turn into a freezer tray and freeze for 1 hour.

Remove from the freezer, place in the processer bowl and process for 3–5 seconds to break down any large ice crystals.

Return to the tray and freeze until firm.

Serve scooped with fan wafers and decorated with sliced kiwi fruit if liked.

Apple mint sorbet

Serves: 6
Attachments: metal blade, whipping blade (optional)

450g/1lb dessert apples, peeled and cored
300ml/½ pint water
100g/4oz granulated sugar
6 tablespoons white wine
4 tablespoons sweet mint jelly
2 egg whites

Fit the metal blade. Place the apples in the processor bowl and process until coarsely chopped. Place in a pan with the water and sugar and cook, covered, for 20 minutes, until pulpy. Return to the processor bowl with the wine and mint jelly and process until smooth.

Pour into a freezer tray and freeze for 1 hour or until semi-frozen. Return to the processor bowl and process until free of large ice crystals. Transfer to a bowl. Rinse the processor bowl.

Fit the whipping blade, if available, and whip the egg whites until stiff. Alternatively whisk until they stand in stiff peaks. Fold into the apple purée mixture with a metal spoon. Return to the freezer tray and freeze until firm.

Serve the sorbet in scoops with apple slices and mint sprigs if liked.

Viennese mandarin slice

Serves: 6–8
Attachments: metal blade, whipping blade (optional)

225g/8oz margarine, diced
50g/2oz caster sugar
1 teaspoon vanilla essence
225g/8oz plain flour
1 × 300g/11oz can mandarin oranges, drained
300ml/½ pint double cream
25g/1oz flaked toasted almonds

Fit the metal blade. Place the margarine, sugar, vanilla essence
and flour in the processor bowl and process until light and
fluffy, about 20 seconds. Spoon into a piping bag fitted with a
large star nozzle. Pipe 14 'fingers', 7.5cm/3in in length, close
together, side by side, on to a greased baking tray. Repeat twice
to make 3 rectangles the same size. Bake in a preheated
moderately hot oven (200°C, 400°F, gas mark 6) for 20 minutes,
or until golden brown. Cool on the baking trays. Rinse the
processor bowl.

Fit the metal blade. Place half of the mandarins in the
processor bowl and process for ½ second to chop. Remove and
set aside.

Fit the whipping blade, if available. Whip the cream in the
processor until just thick, or alternatively whisk until the cream
stands in soft peaks. Combine the chopped oranges with two-
thirds of the cream.

Carefully lift one shortcake rectangle on to a serving plate.
Spread with half of the cream and mandarin mixture. Top with
a second shortcake rectangle and the remaining cream and
mandarin mixture. Finally top with the third shortcake
rectangle.

Decorate the top with swirls of the remaining cream, the
remaining whole mandarins and flaked almonds.

Chocolate profiteroles

Serves: 4–6
Attachments: metal blade, whipping blade (optional)

sweet choux pastry (see page 120)
300ml/½ pint double cream
125g/4½oz plain chocolate
25g/1oz caster sugar
300ml/½ pint water

Fit the metal blade. Make the sweet choux pastry as on page 120. Place in a piping bag fitted with a large plain nozzle and pipe small rounds on to a greased baking tray.

Bake in a preheated hot oven (220°C, 425°F, gas mark 7) for 15–20 minutes until crisp and dry. Remove from the oven and pierce each profiterole with a sharp knife to release any steam.

Fit the whipping blade, if used, and whip the cream until thick. Alternatively, whisk the cream until it stands in firm peaks. Split each profiterole in half and fill with the cream. Sandwich the halves back together again and place in a serving dish.

To make the sauce, melt the chocolate in a bowl over a saucepan of hot water. Boil the water and sugar together in another saucepan for about 5 minutes then add, spoon by spoon, to the chocolate. Simmer for a further 5–10 minutes until the chocolate sauce coats the back of a spoon.

Spoon over the profiteroles and serve at once.

Home baking

Shortcrust pastry

Makes: enough pastry for 1 20cm/8in flan, 12 double-crust tartlets, 4 small savoury pies, 4 small Cornish pasties or 1 large pie crust.
Attachment: metal blade

225g/8oz plain flour

¼ teaspoon salt
100g/4oz butter, cut into pieces
2 tablespoons iced water

Fit the metal blade. Place the flour, salt and butter in the processor and process for 7–8 seconds or until the mixture resembles fine breadcrumbs.

Add the water, a tablespoon at a time, through the feed tube with the motor running, and process until the ingredients just bind together to make a ball.

Turn on to a lightly-floured surface and knead lightly until smooth and free from cracks. Wrap in polythene or cling film and chill for 15 minutes. Use as required.

Variations

Wholemeal pastry: Prepare as above but use wholemeal flour instead of plain flour.
Cheese pastry: Grate 75g/3oz Cheddar cheese using the grating disc. Prepare as above but add ½ teaspoon dry mustard powder with the flour and salt and add the cheese with the water.
Rich shortcrust pastry: Place 175g/6oz flour, 75g/3oz diced butter and 25g/1oz caster sugar in the processor and process for 7–8 seconds or until the mixture resembles fine breadcrumbs. Add 1 egg yolk and 1 tablespoon iced water through the feed tube with the motor running and process until the ingredients just bind. Continue as above.

Choux pastry

Makes: enough for about 30 profiteroles, 12 eclairs, or 1 puff ring or gougère and 12 puffs
Attachment: metal blade

100g/4oz plain flour
pinch of salt
150ml/¼ pint water
50g/2oz butter
4 eggs

Fit the metal blade. Place the flour and salt in the processor bowl and process for 1 second to blend.

Place the water and butter in a pan and bring slowly to the boil. Quickly add to the flour in the processor bowl, through the feed tube, with the motor running, and process to blend, about 3 seconds.

Add the eggs, one at a time, and process until thick and glossy. Allow to cool slightly then place into a piping bag fitted with a suitable nozzle and use as required.

Variations

Sweet choux pastry: Make as above but add 1 teaspoon caster sugar with the flour.
Ham choux pastry: Make as above but add 50g/2oz chopped ham after adding the eggs.
Herby choux pastry: Make as above but add 2 teaspoons chopped fresh herbs or 1 teaspoon dried after adding the eggs.
Orange or lemon choux pastry: Make as above but add the grated rind of 1 small orange or lemon after adding the eggs.
Bacon choux pastry: Make as above but add 50g/2oz finely-chopped cooked bacon after adding the eggs.
Onion choux pastry: Make as above but add 1 small chopped cooked onion after adding the eggs.

Basic victoria sandwich

Serves: 6
Attachments: metal or plastic blade

125g/4oz self-raising flour
¾ teaspoon baking powder
125g/4oz soft blend margarine
125g/4oz caster sugar
2 eggs
3 tablespoons jam
150ml/¼ pint whipped cream
sifted icing sugar to dust

Fit the metal or plastic blade. Place the flour, baking powder, margarine, sugar and eggs in the processor bowl and process for 10–12 seconds until well blended.

Divide the mixture between 2 greased and base-lined 18cm/7in sandwich tins and level the tops.

Bake in a preheated moderate oven (180°C, 350°F, gas mark 4) for 25–30 minutes or until the tops spring back when lightly touched with the fingertips. Leave to cool in the tins for 2–3 minutes, then transfer to a wire rack to cool completely.

When cold sandwich the cakes together with the jam and cream and dust the top with icing sugar. Cut into wedges to serve.

Basic white bread

Makes: 1 × 450g/1lb loaf or 6 rolls
Attachment: metal blade

½ tablespoon dried yeast
½ teaspoon caster sugar
50ml/2fl oz warm water
50ml/2fl oz warm milk
200g/7oz warm strong plain white flour
¾ teaspoon salt
25g/1oz butter or margarine
beaten egg to glaze
poppy seeds, sesame seeds, rolled oats, cumin seeds, caraway seeds, cracked wheat, etc. to sprinkle (optional)

Place the yeast, sugar, water and milk in a jug, mixing well. Leave in a warm place until frothy, about 10–15 minutes.

Fit the metal blade. Place the warm flour, salt and butter or margarine in the processor bowl and process for 4–5 seconds until well mixed.

With the motor running, add the yeast mixture through the feed tube and process for 25–30 seconds to blend and knead the dough.

Remove and place in an oiled bowl and cover with cling film. Leave to rise in a warm place until doubled in size, about 1–1½ hours.

Return the dough to the processor bowl and process for

10–15 seconds. Shape as required (see below). Cover with cling film and leave to rise in a warm place until doubled in size, about 1 hour.

Glaze with beaten egg and sprinkle with seeds if liked. Bake in a preheated hot oven (220°C, 425°F, gas mark 7) for the times given. Loaves and rolls are cooked when they sound hollow when rapped on the bottom with the knuckles. Allow to cool on a wire rack.

Shaping

Tin loaf: Flatten the dough out to an oblong about 2.5cm/1in thick. Fold in three and tuck in the ends of the seam. Place, seam side down, in a greased 450g/1lb loaf tin. Prove and bake for 25–30 minutes.

Plait: Divide the dough into three equal pieces. Roll each into a long strand. Starting at the centre, plait the strands loosely together down to one end. Dampen the end of each strand and pinch together to seal. Plait the other end the same way. Prove and bake for 25–30 minutes.

Round rolls: Divide the dough into 6 equal pieces. Shape into rounds and place well apart on a greased baking tray. Prove and bake for 15–20 minutes.

Finger rolls: Divide the dough into 6 equal pieces. Roll into sausage shapes. Place on a greased baking tray. Prove and bake for 15–20 minutes.

The processor can also be used to make wholemeal bread, which needs a great deal of kneading; see page 142.

Rich celebration fruit cake

Makes: 1 × 23cm/9in round cake
Attachment: metal blade

rind of ½ lemon
350g/12oz butter, diced
350g/12oz soft brown sugar
6 large eggs
400g/14oz plain flour

1 teaspoon ground mixed spice
1 teaspoon cinnamon
625g/1lb 6oz currants
225g/8oz sultanas
225g/8oz raisins
175g/6oz glacé cherries, halved
100g/4oz chopped mixed peel
100g/4oz flaked almonds
2 tablespoons brandy

Fit the metal blade. Place the lemon rind in the processor bowl and process for 5 seconds to chop. Add the butter, sugar, eggs, flour and spices. Process for about 20 seconds until well mixed.

Remove from the bowl and fold in the dried fruit, cherries, peel, nuts and brandy, mixing well. It is often better to do this by hand since most processors cannot cope with such a large quantity, although if you do have a catering size processor, add the fruit, nuts and brandy and process for 3–4 seconds to mix.

Spoon into a greased and lined 23cm/9in round cake tin. Make a slight hollow in the centre to enable the cake to rise evenly and bake in a preheated cool oven (150°C, 300°F, gas mark 1) for 4 hours, or until a skewer inserted into the centre of the cake comes out clean.

Allow to cool slightly in the tin, then transfer to a wire rack to cool completely. Decorate with almond paste (see page 151) and royal icing (see page 151) if liked.

Wholemeal walnut pie

Serves: 6
Attachments: metal blade, plastic blade

225g/8oz wholemeal pastry (see page 119)
rind of 2 lemons
175g/6oz butter
225g/8oz muscovado sugar
3 eggs
juice of 1½ lemons
225g/8oz walnut halves

Fit the metal blade. Prepare the wholemeal pastry as on page 119. Chill for 15 minutes.

Place the lemon rind in the processor bowl and process until finely chopped.

Fit the plastic blade. Add the butter, sugar, eggs and lemon juice to the rind and process until well blended, about 8–10 seconds.

Add the walnut halves and process for 2 seconds to mix.

Line a 20cm/8in greased flan tin with the pastry and bake 'blind' in a preheated moderate oven (180°C, 350°F, gas mark 4) for 10 minutes.

Spoon the walnut mixture into the flan and continue to cook for 45 minutes until the filling is well-risen and browned. Serve warm or cold with cream.

Lemon and almond flan

Serves: 6
Attachment: metal blade

175g/6oz rich shortcrust pastry (see page 119)

Topping:
juice of 2 lemons
100g/4oz caster sugar
sliced flesh of 3 lemons

Filling:
rind of 1 lemon
50g/2oz butter
50g/2oz caster sugar
25g/1oz flour
50g/2oz ground almonds
1 egg

Fit the metal blade. Prepare the rich shortcrust pastry as on page 119. Chill for 15 minutes. Line a 20cm/8in greased flan tin with the pastry and bake 'blind' in a preheated moderately hot oven (200°C, 400°F, gas mark 6) for 5 minutes. Rinse the processor bowl.

Meanwhile, place the lemon juice and sugar in a pan. Bring to the boil, add the lemon slices and simmer for 5 minutes. Allow to cool.

Fit the metal blade. Place the lemon rind in the processor bowl and process until finely chopped. Add the butter, sugar, flour, almonds and egg, and process until smooth and blended, about 8 seconds.

Spread the almond mixture in the pastry case. Reduce the oven temperature to 190°C, 375°F, gas mark 5 and bake the flan for 30 minutes until golden brown.

Allow to cool then arrange the lemon slices in the syrup attractively over the almond flan. Chill before serving.

Spicy curd lattice pie

Serves: 6
Attachment: metal blade

150g/5oz wholemeal flour
½ teaspoon ground cinnamon
75g/3oz butter, diced
50g/2oz caster sugar
50g/2oz ground almonds
2 egg yolks
350g/12oz lemon curd

Fit the metal blade. Place the flour, cinnamon and butter in the processor bowl and process for 7–8 seconds or until the mixture resembles fine breadcrumbs.

Add the sugar and ground almonds and process for 2 seconds to blend. Add the egg yolks and process until the ingredients just bind together to make a ball.

Roll out two-thirds of the pastry and use to line a 20cm/8in flan ring or loose-bottomed sandwich tin. Fill with the lemon curd.

Roll out the remaining pastry and cut into 1cm/½in strips and use to make a lattice over the lemon curd filling.

Bake in a preheated moderately hot oven (190°C, 375°F, gas mark 5) for 30 minutes. Leave to cool in the tin before removing to serve.

Simple rich chocolate cake

Makes: 1 × 20cm/8in sandwich cake
Attachments: metal or plastic blade

225g/8oz margarine
250g/9oz molasses sugar
4 eggs
175g/6oz self-raising flour
50g/2oz cocoa powder
100ml/4fl oz corn oil

Icing:
50g/2oz butter
4 tablespoons cocoa powder
3 tablespoons milk
150g/5oz sifted icing sugar

Fit the metal blade. Place the margarine and sugar in the processor bowl and process until well blended, about 3 seconds. Add the eggs, flour and cocoa powder and process for a further 3 seconds.

With the motor running, add the corn oil through the feed tube and process until well blended, about 5 seconds.

Spoon the mixture equally into 2 greased and lined 20cm/8in sandwich tins and level the surfaces. Bake in a preheated moderate oven (180°C, 350°F, gas mark 4) for 35 minutes. Cool on a wire rack.

Meanwhile, melt the butter in a pan. Add the cocoa powder, milk and icing sugar, blending well. Remove from the heat and leave to cool and thicken.

Use half of the icing to sandwich the cakes together. Spread the remainder on top of the cake and swirl to give a decorative effect.

Spiced banana cake

Serves: 4–6
Attachment: metal blade

Cake:
100g/4oz butter, diced

100g/4oz soft brown sugar
2 eggs
175g/6oz self-raising flour
1½ teaspoons ground cinnamon
2 ripe bananas, peeled and roughly chopped

Cream cheese frosting:
100g/4oz cream cheese
50g/2oz icing sugar
1 tablespoon lemon juice

Fit the metal blade. Place all the cake ingredients in the processor bowl and process until smooth, about 10 seconds. Spoon into a greased and lined 18cm/7in round cake tin. Bake in a preheated moderate oven (180°C, 350°F, gas mark 4) for 35–40 minutes. Leave to stand in the tin for 3 minutes before turning out on to a wire rack to cook.

Meanwhile, rinse the processor bowl and fit the metal blade. Place the frosting ingredients in the processor bowl and process for about 7 seconds. Using a spatula, push the mixture down into the bowl and process for a further 5–10 seconds until smooth. Chill while the cake is cooking (this can be done in the processor bowl).

Swirl the frosting decoratively on top of the cake using a palette knife. Cut into wedges to serve.

Passion cake

Makes: 1 heart-shaped cake
Attachments: grating disc, metal blade

Cake:
175g/6oz carrots, peeled
50g/2oz walnuts
2 ripe bananas, peeled
275g/10oz plain flour
1 teaspoon bicarbonate of soda
2 teaspoons baking powder
1 teaspoon salt
175g/6oz brown sugar
175ml/6fl oz corn oil
3 eggs

Filling and frosting:
175g/6oz icing sugar
75g/3oz cream cheese
175g/6oz butter
½ teaspoon vanilla essence
100g/4oz walnuts

Fit the grating disc. Grate the carrots through the disc and set aside.

Fit the metal blade. Place the walnuts in the processor bowl and process until chopped. Remove and set aside.

Place the bananas in the processor bowl and process until smooth. Add the flour, soda, baking powder, salt, sugar, oil, eggs and carrots and process until well blended, about 10 seconds. Add the walnuts and process for 2 seconds to blend.

Grease and line 2 shallow heart-shaped tins and divide the cake mixture evenly between them. Cook in a preheated moderate oven (180°C, 350°F, gas mark 4) for about 40 minutes until well-risen and firm to the touch. Cool on a wire rack. Rinse the processor bowl.

Fit the metal blade. Place the icing sugar, cream cheese, butter and vanilla essence in the processor bowl and process until smooth. Use one-quarter to sandwich the two cakes together.

Use half of the remaining frosting to coat the sides of the cake and the remaining half to swirl on top. Wash the processor bowl.

Fit the metal blade. Place the walnuts in the processor bowl and process until finely chopped. Press on to the sides of the cake. Serve lightly chilled.

Apricot cake

Makes: 1 × 18cm/7in cake
Attachment: metal blade

1 × 190g/7½oz can apricot halves, drained
100g/4oz margarine
100g/4oz light muscovado sugar
2 large eggs
175g/6oz self-raising flour
225g/8oz mixed dried fruit
1 tablespoon Demerara sugar

Fit the metal blade. Place the apricot halves in the processor bowl and process for 1 second to chop. Remove and set aside.

Place the margarine, sugar, eggs and flour in the processor bowl and process until smooth and creamy, about 10 seconds.

Add the apricots and dried fruit and process for 2 seconds to mix.

Spoon into a greased and lined 18cm/7in round cake tin and sprinkle with the Demerara sugar. Bake in a preheated moderate oven (160°C, 325°F, gas mark 3) for about 1½ hours. Turn out to cool on a wire rack.

Honeyed fig loaf

Makes: 1 × 450g/1lb loaf
Attachment: metal blade

100g/4oz dried figs
50g/2oz walnuts
250g/9oz self-raising flour
25g/1oz butter
75g/3oz sugar
2 tablespoons clear honey
1 egg
150ml/¼ pint warm milk

Fit the metal blade. Place the figs and walnuts in the processor bowl and process until chopped, about 3–5 seconds. Remove and set aside.

Place the flour and butter in the processor bowl and process until the mixture resembles fine breadcrumbs. Add the sugar, honey, figs and walnuts. With the motor running add the milk through the feed tube and process until well blended, about 5 seconds.

Spoon into a greased 450g/1lb loaf tin and leave to stand for 15 minutes.

Bake in a preheated moderate oven (180°C, 350°F, gas mark 4) for about 50 minutes or until springy to the touch.

Serve warm in slices, with or without butter.

Cheddar scone ring

Makes: 8 scones
Attachments: grating disc, metal blade

50g/2oz Cheddar cheese
225g/8oz self-raising flour
1 teaspoon baking powder
pinch of salt
½ teaspoon dry mustard
50g/2oz butter, diced
about 150ml/¼ pint milk

Fit the grating disc. Grate the cheese through the disc, remove and set aside.

Fit the metal blade. Place the flour, baking powder, salt, mustard and butter in the processor bowl and process for 5 seconds or until well mixed and blended.

With the motor running, add the milk through the feed tube and process to form a soft dough.

Knead lightly on a floured surface and divide into 8 equal portions. Shape each portion into a ball.

Place one ball in the centre of a 20cm/8in greased round cake tin. Arrange the remaining balls around it, just touching.

Brush with milk and bake in a preheated moderately hot oven

(200°C, 400°F, gas mark 6) for about 25 minutes or until well-risen and golden. Serve warm and generously buttered.

Honey and ginger nuts

Makes: about 40
Attachment: metal blade

225g/8oz self-raising flour
pinch of salt
1 teaspoon ground ginger
100g/4oz butter or margarine, diced
100g/4oz soft brown sugar
1 tablespoon creamed honey
1 egg, beaten

Fit the metal blade. Place the flour, salt, ginger and butter in the processor bowl and process until the mixture resembles fine breadcrumbs, about 5 seconds.

Add the sugar, honey and egg and process to make a stiff dough, about 4 seconds. Roll into a large sausage shape, about 4cm/1½in in diameter, on a lightly-floured surface. Cut into about 40 slices and place on greased baking trays about 2.5cm/1in apart.

Bake in a preheated moderate oven (180°C, 350°F, gas mark 4) for about 10–12 minutes. Allow to cool on a wire rack.

Crunchy coconut cookies

Makes: 30
Attachment: metal blade

175g/6oz self-raising flour
100g/4oz porridge oats
100g/4oz desiccated coconut
50g/2oz soft brown sugar
pinch of salt
2 tablespoons creamed honey
100g/4oz margarine
1 egg, beaten

Fit the metal blade. Place the flour, oats, coconut, sugar and salt in the processor bowl and process for 2 seconds to mix.

Melt the honey and margarine in a pan. Cool, slightly, then add with the egg through the feed tube, with the motor running, and process to make a sticky mixture.

Form into 30 cookies, making each from 2 teaspoons of the mixture, and place on greased baking trays, about 4cm/1½in apart. Bake in a cool oven (150°C, 300°F, gas mark 2) for 15 minutes until pale and golden. Cool on a wire rack.

Cranberry nut loaf

Makes: 1 loaf
Attachment: metal blade

rind of 2 oranges
75g/3oz walnut halves
225g/8oz plain flour
1½ teaspoons baking powder
½ teaspoon bicarbonate of soda
1 teaspoon salt
50g/2oz butter, diced
100g/4oz caster sugar
juice of 2 oranges
1 egg
1 × 170g/6oz jar cranberry sauce

Fit the metal blade. Place the orange rind in the processor bowl and process until finely chopped. Add the walnuts and process until coarsely chopped, about 1–2 seconds. Remove and set aside.

Place the flour, baking powder, bicarbonate of soda, salt and butter in the processor bowl and process until the mixture resembles fine breadcrumbs.

Add the sugar, orange juice, orange rind and walnuts, egg and cranberry sauce. Process until well blended, about 3 seconds.

Spoon into a 20 × 10cm/8 × 4in greased and baselined loaf tin. Bake in a preheated moderate oven (180°C, 350°F, gas mark 4) for about 1 hour until risen and browned and when a skewer inserted in to the centre of the cake comes out clean.

Cool on a wire rack. Wrap in foil and store for 2 days before slicing and buttering to serve.

Recipes for infants, toddlers and children

Guide to symbols used in recipes

 Young infant from 0–6 months

 Infant or toddler from 6–18 months

 Toddler 18 months +

Guide to servings

1 cube = early weaners (3–6 months)
2 cubes = 4–6 months
3 cubes = 6–9 months

Banana purée

Serves: 1
Attachment: metal blade

½ very ripe banana
2 teaspoons orange juice or baby's milk

Fit the metal blade. Place the banana and orange juice or baby's milk in the processor bowl and process until smooth.

Serve at once. The unused portion of the banana can be wrapped in cling-film, in the skin, and stored in the refrigerator for up to 2 days.

Baby bolognese

Makes: 18 cubes
Attachment: metal blade

1 small onion, peeled and quartered
350g/12oz chuck steak, cubed
25g/1oz butter
25g/1oz plain flour
125ml/4fl oz light stock
2 tablespoons tomato purée
175g/6oz cooked pasta

Fit the metal blade. Place the onion in the processor bowl and process until chopped, about 5 seconds. Remove and set aside.

Place the beef in the processor bowl and process until minced, about 6–8 seconds. Rinse the processor bowl.

Melt the butter in a pan. Add the onion and cook for 5 minutes. Stir in the beef and cook, stirring frequently, for a further 5 minutes.

Add the flour, blending well. Cook for 1 minute. Gradually add the stock and tomato purée, blending well. Cover and cook for 25 minutes, stirring occasionally.

Stir the cooked pasta into the sauce, blending well. Pour into the processor bowl and process to chop to desired smooth or chunky consistency (according to age). Serve warm. Freeze the remainder in sterilized ice cube trays.

Banana and cottage cheese surprise

Serves: 1
Attachment: metal blade

1 ripe banana, peeled
50g/2oz cottage cheese
4 tablespoons fresh orange juice
1 teaspoon honey (optional)

Fit the metal blade. Place the banana in the processor bowl and process until very coarsely puréed, about 2 seconds.

Add the cottage cheese, orange juice and honey if used. Process for 2 seconds then serve at once.

Variations

The banana may be replaced with melon, pineapple or mango if liked.

Orange yoghurt dessert

Serves: 2–3
Attachment: metal blade

juice of 2 oranges
2 teaspoons powdered gelatine
100ml/4fl oz hot water
2 teaspoons clear honey
150ml/¼ pint natural yoghurt

Place the orange juice in a measuring jug and make up to 200ml/7fl oz with water if necessary.

Dissolve the gelatine in the hot water then add the honey, stirring to blend. Mix with the orange juice.

Fit the metal blade. Place the yoghurt in the processor bowl and add the orange mixture. Process for 3–4 seconds to blend.

Pour into individual serving dishes and chill until set, about 4 hours.

Serve with slices of orange if liked.

Cauliflower cheese

Serves: 1
Attachments: grating disc, metal blade

25g/1oz Edam cheese
25g/1oz brown bread, cubed
75–100g/3–4oz cauliflower florets

Fit the grating disc. Grate the cheese through the disc and set aside.

Fit the metal blade. With the motor running, add the bread through the feed tube and process to make breadcrumbs.

Cook the cauliflower florets in boiling, unsalted water for about 7 minutes, or until tender. Drain, reserving the cooking liquor.

Add the cheese to the breadcrumbs in the processor bowl and add 4 tablespoons of the cooking liquor. Process for about 4 seconds or until the cheese melts.

Add the cooked cauliflower and process further until roughly puréed, about 3–4 seconds. Serve warm.

Nesting egg

Serves: 1
Attachment: metal blade

1 teaspoon butter
1 small potato, peeled and cooked
2 teaspoons cottage cheese
1 egg

Grease the base and sides of a small ramekin dish with a little of the butter.

Fit the metal blade. Place the potato and cottage cheese in the processor bowl and process until smooth, about 5 seconds. Remove and spoon into the prepared dish.

Make a hollow in the centre of the potato to make a 'nest' for the egg. Carefully crack the egg into the hollow and dot with the remaining butter.

Bake in a preheated moderate oven (180°C, 350°F, gas mark 4) for about 15 minutes or until the egg is set.

Variation

Older children may appreciate the addition of a little cooked, chopped spinach to their egg nest and a little grated cheese sprinkled over the top prior to cooking.

Roast meat dinner

Makes: 12 cubes
Attachment: metal blade

175g/6oz lean roast meat, cubed or sliced
350g/12oz freshly-cooked vegetables, cooked without salt
thin gravy, stock or vegetable cooking liquor

This is the ideal meal for infants, toddlers and young children to try to encourage eating with the rest of the family. Use roast meat from the family joint, like beef, lamb, pork, chicken or veal. Vegetables like carrots, peas, beans, cauliflower, swedes and leeks made ideal partners. This recipe makes 12 deep cubes of food and can be frozen in a sterilized ice cube tray for further meals. Early weaners should start with just 1 cube and the mixture should be finely puréed. Older infants and toddlers can have 2–3 cubes of coarsely puréed or chopped food.

Fit the metal blade. Place the meat and vegetables in the processor bowl and process to desired consistency, about 5–10 seconds.

Add sufficient thin gravy, stock or vegetable cooking liquor to make the desired consistency, and process for a further 2 seconds. Serve warm.

Note: To use frozen cubes, defrost, covered, at room temperature then thoroughly reheat until boiling. Allow to cool to desired temperature to serve.

Lucy's liver

Serves: 2
Attachments: slicing disc, metal blade

1 small carrot, peeled
1 small potato, peeled and halved
175ml/6fl oz light stock
225g/8oz calf's or chicken liver
1 tomato, peeled

My daughter Lucy doesn't hate, but doesn't love, liver – cooked
and processed this way, however, it has become a favourite meal.

Fit the slicing disc. Slice the carrot and potato through the disc
and place in a saucepan. Add the stock and cook until tender,
about 10 minutes.

Add the liver and cook for a further 4–5 minutes.

Fit the metal blade. Place the liver mixture into the processor
bowl and add the tomato. Process until smooth or finely
chopped – adding a little extra stock if the consistency is too dry.
Serve warm, or allow to cool and serve with toast, as a spread.

Chocolate and orange fley

Serves: 6
Attachments: whipping blade (optional), plastic or metal blade

3 egg whites
75g/3oz eating chocolate
3 egg yolks
2 teaspoons concentrated orange juice

Chocolate and orange fley is a favourite of Ben and Sam
Zalcman – my two chief tasters for this section. It is not a soufflé,
although similar in texture, more of a mousse.

Fit the whipping blade, if available, and whip the egg whites
until stiff. Alternatively, whisk until they stand in stiff peaks
then place in the processor bowl.

Melt the chocolate in a bowl over a saucepan of hot water.
Spoon into the processor bowl with the egg yolks and orange
juice. Process for just 2 seconds to blend. Spoon into individual

dishes and chill until firm, about 4 hours.

This recipe makes 6 portions or – since it is also enjoyed by adults – it makes 3 adult portions.

Honeyed apple crumble

Serves: 4
Attachments: slicing disc, metal blade

6 dessert apples, peeled, cored and quartered
3–4 tablespoons clear honey
150g/5oz wholemeal flour
25g/1oz wheatgerm
pinch of salt
1 teaspoon ground cinnamon (optional)
50g/2oz butter
50g/2oz brown sugar

Fit the slicing disc. Slice the apples through the disc and place in a greased ovenproof dish. Drizzle over the honey.

Fit the metal blade. Place the flour, wheatgerm, salt, cinnamon (if used) and butter in the processor bowl and process until the mixture resembles fine breadcrumbs, about 6 seconds. Add the sugar and process for a further 2 seconds to mix.

Spoon over the apple mixture, smoothing the surface. Bake in a preheated moderately hot oven (190°C, 375°F, gas mark 5) for 30 minutes. Serve with a little pouring custard.

Bean pizza squares

Makes: 9
Attachments: grating disc, metal blade

75g/3oz Cheddar cheese, cubed
175g/6oz self-raising flour
pinch of salt
40g/1½oz butter, diced
1 egg
1–2 tablespoons milk
1 × 450g/1lb can baked beans in tomato sauce
4 tablespoons sweetcorn kernels
3 tomatoes, thinly sliced

Fit the grating disc. Grate the cheese through the disc and set aside.

Fit the metal blade. Place the flour, salt and butter in the processor bowl and process until the mixture resembles fine breadcrumbs, about 5–7 seconds.

With the motor running, add the egg and milk through the feed tube and process until the mixture forms a smooth dough, about 4 seconds.

Roll out on a floured surface to a 23cm/9in square. Place on a greased baking sheet and brush with a little oil. Cover with the baked beans, making sure they reach the edges. Sprinkle with the sweetcorn kernels.

Arrange the tomatoes on top and sprinkle with the grated cheese. Bake in a preheated hot oven (220°C, 425°F, gas mark 7) for about 25 minutes, or until the scone base has risen and the top is lightly golden. Serve hot, cut into squares or fingers.

Healthy eating and slimming

'Healthfood' loaf

Serves: 4
Attachments: metal blade, slicing disc, grating disc

100g/4oz wholemeal bread, cubed
15g/½oz fresh parsley
100g/4oz hazelnuts
1 × 227g/8oz can tomatoes
1 onion, peeled and quartered
2 cloves garlic, peeled
2 sticks celery, scrubbed
1–2 tablespoons oil
1 tablespoon wholemeal flour
100g/4oz mature Cheddar cheese
2 tablespoons rolled oats
1 egg, beaten
1 teaspoon dried oregano
1 teaspoon salt
freshly ground black pepper
2 bay leaves

Fit the metal blade. Add the bread cubes and parsley through the feed tube with the motor running to make breadcrumbs and chopped parsley. Add the hazelnuts and process until coarsely chopped. Add the tomatoes and process until well blended. Remove from the processor bowl and set aside.

With the metal blade still in position add the onion and garlic and process until chopped. Remove the metal blade and fit the slicing disc. Slice the celery through the disc.

Heat the oil in a large pan and add the onion and celery mixture. Cook until softened, about 3 minutes. Add the flour, blending well.

Fit the grating disc and grate the cheese. Add to the onion mixture with the bread mixture, oats, egg, oregano, salt and pepper to taste. Mix well to blend.

Place the bay leaves in the base of an oiled 450g/1lb loaf tin. Spoon the savoury vegetable and cheese mixture on top and press down well. Cover with greased foil and bake in a preheated moderate oven (180°C, 350°F, gas mark 4) for 1 hour.

Allow to stand in the tin for 10 minutes before turning out to serve. Serve hot or cold, sliced, with salad.

Wholemeal bread

Makes: 1 × 450g/1lb loaf
Attachment: metal blade

½ tablespoon dried yeast
225ml/7½fl oz warm water
½ teaspoon caster sugar
575g/1¼lb warm wholemeal flour
1 teaspoon salt
15g/½oz lard

Place the yeast, half the water and sugar in a jug, mixing well. Leave in a warm place until frothy, about 10–15 minutes.

Fit the metal blade. Place the warm flour, salt and lard in the processor bowl and process for 4–5 seconds until well mixed.

With the motor running, add the yeast mixture and remaining water through the feed tube and process for 25–30 seconds to blend and knead the dough.

Remove and place in an oiled bowl and cover with cling film.

Leave to rise in a warm place until doubled in size, about 1½–2 hours.

Return the dough to the processor bowl and process for 10–15 seconds. Shape into a loaf (see basic white bread page 121) and place in a greased 450g/1lb loaf tin. Cover with clingfilm and leave to rise in a warm place until almost doubled in size, about 1–1½ hours.

Bake in a preheated hot oven (230°C, 450°F, gas mark 8) for 25–30 minutes. When cooked the loaf should sound hollow when tapped on the bottom with the knuckles. Allow to cool on a wire rack.

Wholewheat pasta slaw

Serves: 4
Attachments: slicing disc, grating disc, metal blade

225g/8oz wholewheat pasta
225g/8oz white cabbage, cored
4 sticks celery
3 carrots, peeled
½ large Spanish onion, peeled
150ml/¼ pint natural yoghurt
salt and freshly ground black pepper

Cook the pasta in boiling salted water according to the packet instructions. Drain and allow to cool.

Fit the slicing disc. Cut the cabbage to fit the feed tube and slice the cabbage through the disc. Slice the celery through the disc. Remove and set aside.

Fit the grating disc. Grate the carrots through the disc. Remove and set aside.

Fit the metal blade. Place the onion in the processor bowl and process to chop finely, about 5 seconds.

Add the pasta, cabbage, celery, carrots, yoghurt and salt and pepper to taste. Process for 2–3 seconds to mix. Chill lightly before serving.

Cracked wheat salad

Serves: 4
Attachment: metal blade

100g/4oz cracked wheat
3 spring onions, trimmed
50g/2oz parsley sprigs
50g/2oz mint sprigs
2 tablespoons olive oil
2 tablespoons lemon juice
salt and freshly ground black pepper
black olives and sliced tomatoes to garnish

Place the cracked wheat in a bowl and cover with cold water. Leave to soak for about 30 minutes, drain, then wrap in a tea towel or piece of muslin and squeeze to extract as much liquid as possible.

Fit the metal blade. Place the spring onions in the processor bowl and process until chopped, about 4 seconds. Remove and set aside.

Place the parsley and mint in the processor bowl and process until finely chopped, about 8–10 seconds.

Add the cracked wheat, spring onions, oil, lemon juice, and salt and pepper to taste and process for about 2–4 seconds to mix.

Spoon into a shallow serving dish and garnish with black olives and slices of tomato. Serve at room temperature.

Cheesy lentil loaf

Serves: 4–6
Attachments: metal blade, grating disc, slicing disc

75g/3oz stale or day-old brown bread, cubed
3 sprigs fresh parsley
2 onions, peeled and quartered
225g/8oz Cheddar cheese
50g/2oz mushrooms
½ teaspoon ground cloves
1 egg

3 tablespoons double cream
350g/12oz lentils, cooked until tender then drained
salt and freshly ground black pepper
15g/½oz butter
parsley sprigs to garnish

Fit the metal blade. Add the bread cubes through the feed tube, with the motor running, to make breadcrumbs. Add the parsley and process until chopped. Remove the parsley breadcrumbs and set aside.

Place the onions in the processor bowl and process until very finely chopped, about 6–8 seconds. Remove and set aside.

Fit the grating disc and grate the cheese through the disc. Remove and set aside.

Fit the slicing disc. Slice the mushrooms through the disc. Remove and set aside.

Fit the metal disc. Place the cloves, egg and cream in the processor bowl and process for 2 seconds to blend. Add the breadcrumbs, onion, cheese, mushrooms, lentils, and salt and pepper to taste. Process for 4–5 seconds to mix.

Spoon into a well greased 450g/1lb loaf tin. Dot with butter and bake in a moderate oven (180°C, 350°F, gas mark 4) for 45–50 minutes, or until the loaf is firm and a skewer inserted into the centre of the loaf, comes out clean.

Turn out on to a warmed serving dish and garnish with parsley sprigs. Serve sliced with a tomato sauce.

Bean and cheese pancakes

Serves: 4
Attachment: metal blade

Pancake batter (see page 66)
oil for cooking
225g/8oz cottage cheese
2 × 225g/8oz cans curried beans with sultanas
salt and freshly ground black pepper
150ml/¼ pint soured cream
½ teaspoon dried dill

Fit the metal blade. Prepare the pancake batter as on page 66.

Cook the pancakes as on page 66 to make 8 pancakes.

Mix the cottage cheese with the curried beans and sultanas and season with salt and pepper to taste. Divide the mixture between the pancakes and roll up.

Arrange on a greased ovenproof serving dish and cover with foil. Cook in a preheated moderately hot oven (200°C, 400°F, gas mark 6) for about 8 minutes.

Place the soured cream in a small pan and heat until hot but not boiling. Spoon down the centre of the pancakes and sprinkle with the dill. Serve at once.

Wholemeal spaghetti with cottage cheese and almonds

Serves: 4
Attachment: metal blade

2 sprigs fresh parsley
100g/4oz blanched almonds
100g/4oz cottage cheese
25g/1oz grated Parmesan cheese
pinch of ground nutmeg
pinch of ground cinnamon
150ml/¼ pint single cream
3 tablespoons olive oil
salt
350g/12oz wholemeal spaghetti
50g/2oz butter
flaked toasted almonds to garnish

Fit the metal blade. Place the parsley in the processor bowl and process until finely chopped, about 5 seconds. Remove and set aside.

Place the almonds in the processor bowl and process until finely ground, about 10–15 seconds. Add the cottage cheese, Parmesan cheese, nutmeg, cinnamon, cream, oil and salt to taste. Process for about 5–10 seconds to make a thick paste.

Meanwhile, cook the spaghetti in boiling salted water until cooked, about 15 minutes. Drain, reserving 150ml/¼ pint of the cooking liquor.

Toss the spaghetti in the butter and parsley and place in a warmed serving dish.

Add the cooking liquor to the processor and process for 2–3 seconds to blend. Pour over the spaghetti and serve at once, garnished with a few toasted almonds.

Slimmers chilli con carne

Serves: 4
Attachment: metal blade

450g/1lb lean chuck steak
2 onions, peeled
275g/10oz peppers, cored and seeded
1 × 397g/14oz can peeled tomatoes in tomato juice
300ml/½ pint tomato juice
3 tablespoons tomato purée
1 tablespoon red wine vinegar
2–4 teaspoons chilli powder
salt and freshly ground black pepper
1 × 440g/15oz can red kidney beans, drained

Fit the metal blade. Cut the meat into cubes, removing and discarding any fat. Place the meat in the processor bowl and process for 5–6 seconds until minced. Remove and set aside.

Place the onions and peppers in the processor bowl and process until chopped, about 3–5 seconds.

Place the beef in a non-stick pan and fry until lightly browned. Add the onion and peppers and cook for 5 minutes. Add the tomatoes, tomato juice, tomato purée, vinegar, chilli powder and salt and pepper to taste. Mix well to blend, cover and cook for 15–20 minutes.

Add the kidney beans, mixing well. Cook for a further 5 minutes. Serve hot with crispbreads if liked.

Total calories per portion: 345.

Breakfast crunch

Serves: 8
Attachment: metal blade

50g/2oz blanched almonds
100g/4oz dried apricots
100g/4oz dried apple
100g/4oz currants, raisins or sultanas
100g/4oz All Bran or Bran Buds
100g/4oz bran flakes
skimmed milk or natural yoghurt to serve

Fit the metal blade. Place the almonds in the processor bowl and process to chop, about 4 seconds. Remove and set aside.

Place the dried apricots and apples in the processor bowl and process until chopped, about 5 seconds.

Add the currants, raisins or sultanas and All Bran or Bran Buds and process for 3 seconds to mix.

Remove from the bowl and fold in the bran flakes with a spoon. Store in an airtight jar until required.

Serve with a little skimmed milk or yoghurt.

Calories per serving: 210.

Creamy mackerel dip crunch

Serves: 4
Attachment: metal blade

350g/12oz smoked mackerel fillets, skinned
3 tablespoons lemon juice
175ml/6fl oz natural yoghurt
freshly ground pepper
salad crudités to serve (carrot sticks, pepper sticks, whole mushrooms, cauliflower florets or cucumber slices, for example)

Fit the metal blade. Place the mackerel, lemon juice, yoghurt and pepper to taste in the processor bowl and process until smooth, about 10 seconds.

Serve in a bowl surrounded with salad crudités as a starter or hors d'oeuvres.

Calories per serving: about 280.

Not so sinful strawberry mousse

Serves: 4
Attachments: metal blade, whipping blade (optional)

225g/8oz strawberries, hulled
150ml/¼ pint natural yoghurt
liquid sweetener to taste (optional)
15g/½oz powdered gelatine
2 tablespoons water
2 egg whites
4 whole strawberries to decorate

Fit the metal blade. Place the strawberries and yoghurt in the processor bowl and process until smooth, about 10 seconds. Add liquid sweetener to taste if liked.

Dissolve the gelatine in the water and add to the strawberry mixture. Process for 2 seconds to blend. Remove and rinse the processor bowl.

Fit the whipping blade if available and whip the egg whites until stiff. Alternatively whisk the egg whites until they stand in firm peaks. Fold into the strawberry mixture with a metal spoon.

Spoon into 4 small dessert dishes and chill until firm. Decorate each with a whole strawberry before serving.

Calories per serving: 50.

Frozen hazelnut and banana yoghurt

Serves: 6
Attachments: metal blade, whipping blade (optional)

rind of 1 lemon
50g/2oz toasted hazelnuts
4 ripe bananas, peeled
juice of 1 lemon
1 tablespoon brown rum
300ml/½ pint natural yoghurt
2 tablespoons soft brown sugar
2 egg whites

Fit the metal blade. Place the lemon rind in the processor bowl and process until finely chopped, about 5 seconds.

Add the hazelnuts and process until chopped, about 4 seconds.

Add the bananas, lemon juice, rum, yoghurt and sugar and process until almost smooth, about 8 seconds. Remove and rinse the processor bowl.

Fit the whipping blade, if available. Whip the egg whites until stiff. Alternatively, whisk until the egg whites stand in stiff peaks. Add to the banana mixture and process for 2 seconds to blend.

Pour into a freezer tray and freeze until half-frozen.

Return to the processor bowl and process for 2 seconds to break down any ice crystals. Return to the freezer and freeze until firm. Serve in scoops.

Calories per serving: 140.

Preserves and confectionery

Almond paste

Makes: enough to cover 1 × 23cm/9in round cake
Attachment: metal blade

400g/14oz blanched almonds
200g/7oz icing sugar
200g/7oz caster sugar
2 eggs
½ teaspoon almond essence
1 teaspoon lemon juice

Fit the metal blade. Place the almonds in the processor bowl and process until finely ground, about 25–35 seconds.

Add the sugars, eggs, almond essence and lemon juice and process until the mixture makes a smooth ball, about 10 seconds. Cover and chill before using as required.

Royal icing

Makes: enough to cover 1 × 23cm/9in round cake
Attachments: metal or plastic blade

4 egg whites
2 teaspoons glycerine
900g/2lb sifted icing sugar

Fit the metal or plastic blade. Place the egg whites in the processor bowl and process for 2–3 seconds. Add the glycerine and process for a further 2 seconds.

Gradually add the icing sugar, in batches, through the feed tube or by removing the lid, and process until smooth, thick and glossy. Use as required.

Red tomato chutney

Makes: about 3.5kg/8lb
Attachment: metal blade

2.75kg/6lb ripe tomatoes
2 large onions, peeled and halved
4 teaspoons whole allspice
1 teaspoon cayenne pepper
1 tablespoon salt
250ml/8fl oz vinegar
350g/12oz brown sugar

Peel and quarter the tomatoes and place in a large pan.

Fit the metal blade. Add the onions to the processor bowl and process until finely chopped. Add to the tomato mixture with the allspice, tied in muslin, pepper and salt. Cook over a gentle heat until pulpy, about 10–15 minutes.

Add the vinegar and sugar, blending well. Simmer until the mixture thickens, about 40–60 minutes. Remove and discard the allspice in muslin. Pour into clean hot jars, cool, cover and label.

Tomato and pepper relish

Makes: 1.5kg/3lb
Attachment: metal blade

3 red peppers, cored and seeded
3 green peppers, cored and seeded
350g/12oz onions, peeled and quartered
450g/1lb ripe tomatoes, peeled and quartered
225g/8oz demerara sugar
475ml/16fl oz malt vinegar

1 teaspoon ground allspice
1 teaspoon mustard seeds
2 teaspoons black peppercorns

Fit the metal blade. Place the peppers in the processor bowl and process until chopped, about 5 seconds. Remove and place in a large pan.

Add the onion to the processor bowl and process until chopped, about 5 seconds. Remove and add to the peppers with the tomatoes, sugar and vinegar. Heat until the sugar dissolves.

Tie the allspice, mustard seeds and black peppercorns in a muslin bag and add to the pan. Simmer gently for about 1½ hours until thick and pulpy. Remove and discard the muslin bag.

Pour into warmed, sterilized jars, cover, seal, label and store. Use after 2–3 months.

Rhubarb and raisin chutney

Makes: about 1.75kg/4lb
Attachment: metal blade

2 onions, peeled and halved
450g/1lb rhubarb, trimmed
225g/8oz muscovado sugar
300ml/½ pint cider vinegar
150ml/¼ pint water
½ teaspoon allspice
½ teaspoon whole cloves
½ teaspoon salt
1 teaspoon mustard seeds
¼ teaspoon celery seeds
225g/8oz raisins

Fit the metal blade. Place the onion and rhubarb in the processor bowl and process until coarsely chopped.

Place the sugar, vinegar, water and spices in a heavy-based pan, bring to the boil and boil for 5 minutes.

Add the onion and rhubarb mixture and simmer gently for 45 minutes.

Add the raisins and continue cooking, uncovered, until thick, stirring occasionally.

Pour into clean hot jars, cool, cover and label.

Apple and molasses chutney

Makes: about 3.25kg/7lb
Attachment: metal blade

2 cloves garlic, peeled
1.75kg/4lb cooking apples, peeled, cored and quartered
600ml/1 pint vinegar
675g/1½lb molasses sugar
2 teaspoons ground ginger
½ teaspoon mixed spice
½ teaspoon salt
pinch of cayenne pepper

Fit the metal blade. Place the garlic in the processor bowl and process until finely chopped. Add half the apples and process until coarsely chopped. Place in a large pan. Add the remaining apples to the processor bowl and process until coarsely chopped. Add to the pan with half of the vinegar. Cook until thick and pulpy.

Add the remaining vinegar, sugar, ginger, mixed spice, salt and cayenne pepper. Cook for a further 20 minutes until thick.

Pour into clean hot jars, cool, cover and label.

Brandy mincemeat

Makes: about 4kg/9lb
Attachments: grating disc, metal blade

1kg/2lb cooking apples, peeled, cored and quartered
350g/12oz carrots, peeled
50g/2oz blanched almonds
225g/8oz cut mixed peel
675g/1½lb currants
675g/1½lb sultanas
350g/12oz shredded suet
675g/1½lb sugar
1½ teaspoons ground mixed spice
1 teaspoon ground nutmeg
150ml/¼ pint brandy

Fit the grating disc. Grate the apples and carrots through the disc. Remove and place in a bowl.

Fit the metal blade. Place the almonds in the processor bowl and process for about 4 seconds to chop. Remove and add to the apple mixture.

Mix the peel with the currants, sultanas and suet. Place one-third of the mixture into the processor bowl and process for 10 seconds. Remove and add to the apple mixture. Repeat with the remaining fruit mixture, processing in 2 batches.

Add the sugar, spices and brandy and mix well. Pack into clean sterilized jars and cover with an airtight seal. Store for up to 6 weeks.

Chocolate honey truffles

Makes: 24
Attachment: metal blade

225g/8oz sponge cake
50g/2oz walnuts, toasted hazelnuts or almonds
3 tablespoons cocoa powder
4 tablespoons set or creamed honey
1–2 tablespoons orange juice or brown rum
cocoa powder, drinking chocolate or coconut to coat

Fit the metal blade. Place the sponge cake and nuts in the processor bowl and process until the cake is crumbed and nuts are chopped, about 5–8 seconds.

Add the cocoa powder, honey, and orange juice or rum and process until the mixture binds to a firm ball, about 5 seconds. Divide into about 24 pieces and roll each into a small ball.

Roll to coat in cocoa powder, drinking chocolate or coconut. Chill until required.

Drinks

Quick lemon squash

Makes: 600ml/1pt
Attachment: metal blade

1 lemon, quartered
2 tablespoons sugar
6 ice cubes
300ml/½ pint water
1 lemon, sliced

Fit the metal blade. Place the unpeeled lemon quarters in the processor with the sugar, ice cubes and water. Process for no more than 10 seconds.

Strain into a jug and add the sliced lemon. Serve chilled.

Strawberry yoghurt shake

Makes: 1 large glass
Attachment: metal blade

250g/9oz natural yoghurt
225g/8oz strawberries, hulled
3 teaspoons clear honey
mint leaves and a whole strawberry to decorate

Fit the metal blade. Place the yoghurt, strawberries and honey in the processor bowl and process until smooth and frothy, about 8 seconds.

Pour into a chilled glass and decorate with mint leaves and a whole strawberry.

Banana milkshake

Serves: 2
Attachment: metal blade

450ml/¾ pint cold milk
1 large banana, peeled
2 scoops vanilla ice cream
ground nutmeg to dust

Fit the metal blade. Place the milk, banana and ice cream in the processor bowl and process until smooth and frothy, about 10–15 seconds.

Pour into two tall glasses and serve immediately with straws and dusted with a little ground nutmeg.

Variations

Strawberry milkshake Make as above but use strawberry flavour ice cream and 8 strawberries, instead of the banana and vanilla ice cream. Omit the nutmeg.
Coffee milkshake Make as above but dissolve 2 teaspoons instant coffee powder and 2 teaspoons sugar in a little hot water and use instead of the banana. Use coffee-flavoured ice cream instead of the vanilla. Omit the nutmeg and serve with a chocolate flake sprinkled over the top.

Chocolate milkshake Make as above but use 1½ tablespoons drinking chocolate and chocolate-flavoured ice cream instead of the banana and vanilla ice cream. Omit the nutmeg.

Raspberry milkshake Make as above but use 75g/3oz fresh hulled raspberries and raspberry or strawberry ice cream. Omit the nutmeg.

Malted milkshake Make as above but use 1½ tablespoons malt extract instead of the banana.

Pina colada

Serves: 1
Attachment: metal blade

2 measures white rum
2 measures pineapple juice
2 teaspoons coconut milk or meat
2 dashes angostura bitters
5 ice cubes
pineapple slices and a maraschino cherry to decorate

Fit the metal blade. Place the rum, pineapple juice, coconut milk or meat, bitters and ice in the processor bowl and process until smooth, about 10–15 seconds.

Pour into a cocktail glass and decorate with pineapple slices speared with a maraschino cherry.

Alternatively the drink may be served in a hollowed-out pineapple or coconut shell and served with straws.

Ocho rios

Serves: 1
Attachment: metal blade

1 measure dark rum
½ guava, peeled
¼ measure lime juice
ice

Fit the metal blade. Place the rum, guava, lime juice and a few cubes of ice in the processor bowl. Process until smooth, about 4 seconds.

Pour into a chilled champagne glass to serve.

Havana beach

Serves: 1
Attachment: metal blade

½ fresh lime, diced
1 measure white rum
1 teaspoon sugar
ice
ginger ale to top up
lime slices, pineapple slices and a maraschino cherry to decorate

Fit the metal blade. Place the lime, rum, sugar and a few cubes of ice in the processor bowl. Process until smooth, about 10 seconds.

Pour into a highball glass and top up with ginger ale.

Decorate with lime and pineapple slices speared with a maraschino cherry.

Fizzgig

Serves: 1
Attachment: metal blade

2 scoops vanilla ice cream
1 measure lime cordial
Coca Cola to top up
fresh fruit slices to decorate
straws to serve

Fit the metal blade. Place the ice cream and lime cordial in the processor bowl and process for 2–3 seconds.

Pour into a highball glass and top up with Coca Cola.

Decorate with slices of fresh fruit and serve with straws.

Amelia

Serves: 1
Attachment: metal blade

2 measures orange juice
10 pineapple cubes
2 ice cubes
ice
1 measure blackcurrant cordial
straws to serve

Fit the metal blade. Place the orange juice, pineapple cubes and ice cubes in the processor bowl and process for 5 seconds.

Pour into a highball glass filled with ice. Carefully pour the blackcurrant cordial on top just before serving. Serve with straws.

Planter's punch

Makes: 8 glasses
Attachment: metal blade

300ml/½ pint dark rum
450ml/¾ pint lemon juice
150ml/¼ pint orange juice
50ml/2fl oz grenadine
8 dashes angostura bitters
ice
soda water to top up
orange and lemon slices to decorate
stirrers and straws to serve

Fit the metal blade. Place the rum, lemon juice, orange juice, grenadine and angostura bitters in the processor bowl and process for 5 seconds.

Divide between 8 glasses filled with cracked ice. Top up with soda water and decorate with orange and lemon slices.

Serve with stirrers and straws.

Bride's bowl

Makes: 30 glasses
Attachment: metal blade

2 × 225g/8oz cans pineapple cubes in sugar syrup
225ml/8fl oz unsweetened pineapple juice
225ml/8fl oz fresh lemon juice
50ml/2fl oz sugar syrup
1 bottle light rum
120ml/4fl oz Drambuie
crushed ice
2 large bottles soda water
900g/2lb strawberries, hulled and sliced
mint sprigs to decorate

Fit the metal blade. Place the pineapple cubes and their juice, pineapple juice, lemon juice, sugar syrup, half of the rum and the Drambuie in the processor bowl and process for 15 seconds. Cover and chill for 24 hours.

To serve, half-fill a large punch bowl with crushed ice. Add the remaining rum and chilled rum mixture. Stir well to blend.

Top up with soda water and add the strawberries. Stir gently then serve decorated with mint sprigs.

White knight

Serves: 1
Attachment: metal blade

½ measure Drambuie
1 measure Malibu coconut liqueur
2 measures pineapple juice
2 ice cubes

Fit the metal blade. Place the Drambuie, Malibu, pineapple juice and ice in the processor bowl and process for 5 seconds.

Pour into a cocktail glass to serve.

Highland tea

Makes: 8 glasses
Attachment: metal blade

120ml/4fl oz Drambuie
225ml/8fl oz vodka
150ml/¼ pint cold weak tea
Coca Cola to top up
stirrers and straws to serve

Fit the metal blade. Place the Drambuie, vodka and tea in the processor bowl and process for 5 seconds.

Pour into highball glasses and top up with Coca Cola. Serve with stirrers and straws.

INDEX

Index

Cook books

☐ **The Infra-Red Cook Book**	Kathy Barnes	£1.50p
☐ **Mrs Beeton's**		
Cookery For All	Mrs Beeton	£3.95p
☐ **The Microwave Cook Book**	Carol Bowen	£1.95p
☐ **Pressure Cooking Day by Day**	Kathleen Broughton	£2.50p
☐ **Middle Eastern Cookery**	A. der Haroutunian	£2.95p
☐ **Vegetarian Cookbook**	Gail Duff	£2.95p
☐ **Crockery Pot Cooking**	Theodora Fitzgibbon	£1.50p
☐ **The Book of Herbs**	Dorothy Hall	£1.95p
☐ **The Best of**	Rosemary Hume and	
Cordon Bleu	Muriel Downes	£1.95p
☐ **Diet for Life**	Mary Laver and	
	Margaret Smith	£1.95p
☐ **Herbs for Health**	Claire Loewenfeld	
and Cookery	and Philippa Back	£2.50p
☐ **The Preserving Book**	Caroline Mackinlay	£4.50p
☐ **The Book of Pies**	Elisabeth Orsini	£1.95p
☐ **Learning to Cook**	Marguerite Patten	£2.50p
☐ **Wild Food**	Roger Phillips	£5.95p
☐ **Complete International**		
Jewish Cookbook	Evelyn Rose	£2.95p
☐ **Caribbean Cookbook**	Rita Springer	£1.95p
☐ **The Times Cookery Book**	} Katie Stewart	£3.50p
☐ **Shortcut Cookery**		£1.95p
☐ **Freezer Cookbook**	Marika Hanbury Tenison	£1.95p
☐ **The Pan Picnic Guide**	Karen Wallace	£1.95p

All these books are available at your local bookshop or newsagent, or
can be ordered direct from the publisher. Indicate the number of copies
required and fill in the form below   11

....

Name_____
(Block letters please)

Address_____

_____

Send to CS Department, Pan Books Ltd, PO Box 40, Basingstoke, Hants
Please enclose remittance to the value of the cover price plus:
35p for the first book plus 15p per copy for each additional book ordered
to a maximum charge of £1.25 to cover postage and packing
Applicable only in the UK

While every effort is made to keep prices low, it is sometimes
necessary to increase prices at short notice. Pan Books reserve
the right to show on covers and charge new retail prices which
may differ from those advertised in the text or elsewhere